Praise for
Marketing Above the Noise
and
Linda J. Popky

"A lot of marketing talk focuses on technology: Twitter, Facebook, viral videos, clicks. Linda Popky understands that technology is an important piece of the puzzle, but not *the* most important piece. Her back-to-basics approach builds on foundational values like trust, relationship-building, and resilience to create customer interest and loyalty. *Marketing Above the Noise* speaks to marketers in their language, but it really shines when the author digs into what specific companies are doing right and wrong."
—Daniel H. Pink, best-selling author of *Drive* and *To Sell Is Human*

"Because of the near infinite amount of information available on the web, buyers now have more information than sellers. It is a new world requiring smart marketers to educate and inform instead of interrupt and sell. Linda Popky shares strategies and tactics that work in this new environment and how to implement them to grow your business."
—David Meerman Scott, best-selling author of ten books including *The New Rules of Marketing and PR*

"It may seem counterintuitive in our new social and digital world, but many aspects of marketing are timeless and still relevant today. In this book, Linda Popky updates these timeless principles with the latest technologies available to marketers. Read this book to ensure your marketing isn't static in the digital era."
—Charlene Li, CEO of Altimeter Group, author of the *New York Times* best-seller *Open Leadership* and co-author of *Groundswell*

"*Marketing Above the Noise* is a tour de force that will help anybody interested in creating marketing dominance to do so in a customer-oriented, highly profitable manner."
—Alan Weiss, best-selling author of *Million Dollar Consulting*

"*Marketing Above the Noise* is required reading for anyone who wants to be more effective at using marketing to reinvent and grow their business. Linda Popky shows us how to take the most essential elements of traditional marketing and apply them in the fast-changing world of social business."

—Dorie Clark, author of *Reinventing You:
Define Your Brand, Imagine Your Future*; adjunct professor,
Duke University Fuqua School of Business

"Stop the marketing madness! If you're a CEO or a CMO who is tired of wasting money on me-too marketing that doesn't work, you must read this book. Linda Popky shows you how to differentiate yourself and a creating a compelling customer-centric strategy that will drive business and make you proud."

—Lisa Earle McLeod, author of *Selling with Noble Purpose*

"Thought provoking and to the point. This book cuts above the noise in the marketing world today."

—Adrian C. Ott, award-winning author and CEO,
The 24-Hour Customer and *Exponential Influence*®

"Want to stand out in today's crowded marketplace? Looking for easy-to-implement marketing strategies that are proven to be effective? In *Marketing Above the Noise*, Linda Popky shares the insider secrets to building buzz that make her Silicon Valley's go-to marketing guru. Get your copy today!"

—Denise Brosseau, CEO, Thought Leadership Lab
and author of *Ready to Be a Thought Leader?*

"This book will change the way you think about your business. In today's membership economy, it's more important than ever that marketers know how to think strategically and stand above the crowd."

—Robbie Kellman Baxter, author of
The Membership Economy

Along with performance, effective marketing is the prerequisite for success. Linda Popky lays out what it takes to succeed. She shows how to get more definitive results from your campaigns, the ways to greater customer engagement, loyalty, and growth. This marketing book is about achieving strategic advantage. Isn't that what it's all about? Master the knowledge in this book and you are on your way."

—Seth Kahan, best-selling author of
Getting Change Right and *Getting Innovation Right*

"In so many cases, when I begin working at the strategic level with companies, they do not know exactly who their customers are, how to engage their prospective customers, and to view marketing in the strategic context where it can catapult a company to its rightful place in the market. Linda makes marketing practical and actionable, using terrific metaphors and stories to make her points so that all executives will want to own this book and leverage its sage advice."

—Janis M. Machala, managing partner, Paladin Partners

"Linda Popky's *Marketing Above the Noise* is a clear message to business leaders on how to market effectively, bring a clear message to customers, and, of course, differentiate from the competitors."

—Brian Geitner, president, NextGear Capital

"With a strategic focus and real world examples, this book shows how to make your marketing program exceptional. Read it, follow Linda's advice, and your marketing program will be outstanding."

—George C. Steinke, CEO, SioTeX Corporation;
Entrepreneur-in-Residence, Texas State University

"Linda Popky understands that you can't change just one thing and expect success; you have to work with your full network and all your organization's resources. *Marketing Above the Noise* provides the strategic guidance you need to quiet the complexity and achieve results."

—Terri Griffith, PhD, Chair of Santa Clara University Management
Department and author of the award-winning book,
*The Plugged-In Manager: Get in Tune with Your People,
Technology, and Organization to Thrive*

"For anyone in the business of getting attention for themselves, their companies, or their products, Popky's book should be on your list. This is a masterful collection of branding and marketing insider knowledge, full of examples from Fortune 500 business issues down to selling snow-cones at the county fair."

—Luke Sullivan, chair of advertising department,
Savannah College of Art and Design

"In her book, Linda Popky addresses one of the nagging questions for post-Twitter marketers: which old-school marketing principles still apply, and which new marketing strategies are essential. She delivers a fresh approach on how to leverage the old with the new to create break-throughs for your brand and your business. *Marketing Above the Noise* is accessible, practical, and results-focused—a must-read not just for marketers, but for anyone in a company who works closely with marketing to create results for the company."

—Kate Purmal, former SVP Digital Content at SanDisk,
now co-founder and COO of CoPilot Systems

"Finally—a book that explains how to market effectively in this new, chaotic world. *Marketing Above the Noise* takes a pragmatic approach to developing effective marketing and advertising campaigns that actually work in today's environment."

—Jeff Johnson, EVP, general manager, Cramer-Krasselt

"I'd like to get this book in the hands of our partners, as well as our marketing team. Linda's common sense approach to marketing is valuable for channel partners, as well as for marketers in general."

—Erna Arnesen, VP Global Channel &
Alliance Marketing, Plantronics

MARKETING
ABOVE THE NOISE

MARKETING
ABOVE THE NOISE

Achieve Strategic Advantage with
MARKETING THAT MATTERS

LINDA J. POPKY

First published by Bibliomotion, Inc.
39 Harvard Street
Brookline, MA 02445
Tel: 617-934-2427
www.bibliomotion.com

Library of Congress Cataloging-in-Publication Data

Popky, Linda J.
  Marketing above the noise : achieve strategic advantage with marketing that matters / Linda J Popky.
      pages cm
  Summary: "In Marketing Above the Noise, Linda Popky has developed an approach to help cut through the clutter, stand out, and effectively build business" — Provided by publisher.
  ISBN 978-1-62956-037-3 (hardback) — ISBN 978-1-62956-038-0 (ebook) — ISBN 978-1-62956-039-7 (enhanced ebook)
  1. Marketing.   I. Title.
  HF5415.P6364 2015
  658.8—dc23
                           2014045353

For my daughter, Ilana

Contents

Foreword

As the founder and CEO of the Chief Customer Officer (CCO) Council, I often find myself at the center of the discussion about the value of marketing in terms of attracting, acquiring, and retaining the most profitable customers.

Today's customer world is a noisy place, full of distractions that organizations have themselves created. The rapacious clamoring for attention, the barrage of new media channels, the audacious claims and celebrity endorsements…are all meant to say, "Pay attention to me!" Faced with a dizzying array of conflicting input and lack of meaningful differentiation, increasingly cynical customers are disconnecting and turning to more relevant customer communities, or ignoring the communications altogether—which causes marketers to shout even louder.

As a result, the marketer's ability to influence customers is hampered, and the ability to influence company strategy is diminishing. Some Chief Marketing Officers (CMOs) are even being replaced by Chief Customer Officers (CCOs), indicating the corporate imperative to focus on the broader customer life cycle rather than strictly upon customer acquisition.

That's why this book is so important. Linda Popky understands that we need to slow down and pay attention to what is truly meaningful. Who are the best customers? What do they need and want—and what are they willing to pay for? What behaviors do they exhibit? What experiences do they desire? How can we use this knowledge to identify the best prospects for the future? How should we set customer strategies for each segment? How do we focus on those customers, channels, and two-way communications vehicles that maximize both customer and business benefit?

Marketers need to refocus on a core tenet: creating profitable, long-term customer relationships. We must drive profitable revenue by understanding and satisfying customer needs more effectively than other competitors. As Linda notes, it isn't about winning awards, creating content that goes viral, being first adopters of a social channel, or getting the most attention in the blogosphere. It is about adding value to both customer and company.

In today's world, value is more than just providing customers with products and services that meet their needs (satisfaction), or even pre-disposing purchase in the face of competitive alternatives (loyalty). It involves extreme customer engagement, where the relationship is so strong that customers will offer their discretionary time for mutual ben-efit. Extreme customer engagement is about involvement—involving your customers in your business and becoming involved in their lives. It begins with formal collaboration to fix problems, shape strategy, and even mutually innovate. It's evidenced by significantly increased willing-ness to advocate, such that you can provide the megaphone and a cus-tomer will happily shout out to those audiences that make the greatest difference in your acquisition and retention efforts.

How do we get there? In this book, Linda advocates a healthy return to the core fundamentals of marketing—a return to guiding principles of strategy used to properly inform marketing decisions. These principles will help businesses more effectively identify customers, create key messages, choose the most effective vehicle, and create meaningful two-way conversa-tions. All this leads to the true goal: driving profitable sales on a sustainable basis. Leveraging these principles will allow marketers to create a timeless marketing growth engine grounded in conversations with, and strategies for, not just any customers but the *right* customers. What we want is to deliver real value in terms of long-term, profitable customer relationships.

Linda draws from her wealth of experience to provide insights that help us understand as marketers where we should be focusing in order to make a difference. Most importantly, in *Marketing Above the Noise*, she puts us on the right path to cut through the noise by listening, tailoring, and delivering what customers truly want. And when businesses do that, everyone wins.

Curtis N. Bingham
CEO, Chief Customer Officer Council

Introduction

"Marketing today has changed almost beyond recognition."
"Today's marketing bears no resemblance to what was done
   previously."
"Technology has totally reinvented marketing."
"Do we even need marketing and marketers anymore?"

The business press and blogs are full of these kinds of headlines about marketing in the twenty-first century. No wonder today's marketers are unsettled! All of this chaos is enough to make marketing professionals seriously question their career choice.

I've been involved with virtually all aspects of marketing over the past thirty years in agencies, corporations, and nonprofits, and as a consultant. During that time, I've seen marketing from just about every angle imaginable. I've seen initiatives that worked well and some that never got out of the gate. I've lived through boom times and budget-slashing recessions. I've also been in the unusual position of managing outstanding marketing campaigns for products that never lived up to their potential.

Having been around the block a few times, I've watched marketing evolve and change dramatically over the years. But I've also watched what *hasn't* changed. And I'm here to tell you that marketing as a profession is alive and well, thank you, but we marketing leaders *do* have some work to do to remain relevant and create value for the organizations that employ us. That's why I wrote this book.

In a world where someone is constantly introducing a new tactic or technique that will "reinvent" the way businesses do marketing, how do you do your job on a day-to-day basis? If there's a presumption that marketing is a simple exercise that almost anyone can do, why is it so hard to have your team do this marketing stuff effectively? In an environment that uses technology to assault our senses, hitting us with more, more, and more stimuli, how do you and your organization stand out from the noise?

It's true that technology has revolutionized marketing. In today's environment, it's fairly simple to create a social media presence. Just about anyone can create a direct marketing campaign. With minimal effort, new products can be launched across a myriad of platforms and devices.

This would be fine if it actually worked across all situations. I can't tell you how many times I see marketing campaigns that have been created and deployed just because someone at a company thought he could. Too often, young, inexperienced executives move forward to execute marketing campaigns without a solid understanding of the fundamentals.

I often find myself telling clients to focus on the parts of their marketing program they should consider cutting out. It's an unusual approach for a marketing consultant, but a few strategic programs done well are more valuable than a whole slew of initiatives that just add more noise to the system. I want to see clients get great results rather than spend more money for a poor return.

Marketing Above the Noise is for marketing leaders who want to understand how to navigate these uncertain waters without risking the gains and successes they've achieved to this point. If you're new to marketing, this book will help you understand the key issues you'll be facing. If you're already a good marketer, reading this book will give you an *even better* understanding of how you can effectively move forward in today's noisy environment. If you're a senior executive, this book will clarify the type of results you can get from your marketing team—and the support they'll require from you to achieve strong results.

The first thing you may notice is that this book is *not* focused on social media, user-generated content, crowdsourcing, digital media, and so on. We'll address many of these tactics, but the core discussion is on starting with a timeless framework—a way of looking at marketing as tied to both business growth and the building and nurturing of ongoing customer engagement. We'll cover:

- The upfront work needed to understand the core imperatives of marketing, including strategy, customers, and markets
- The new realities that have dramatically changed the way we do marketing today
- The momentum factors that will either propel your effort forward within your organization or stop you dead in your tracks
- The reason empowering employees to represent your brand is so critical

Why are these elements so important? With all the attention given to detail, we're losing focus on the bigger picture. We need to ask how marketing can create and grow profitable, sustainable, successful businesses.

It's great to talk about having conversations with customers...but if you haven't done the upfront work to understand your target market, their needs, and where they go for information, then you might be wasting a lot of time and resources having conversations with the wrong people.

It's terrific to invest in a strong set of products or services...but if you don't have consistent, focused messaging that articulates the value customers receive from buying and using your offerings, you're adding overhead and complexity, not clarity.

It's wonderful to have customers engaged with your product and your brand...but if you haven't educated and empowered your employees to represent the brand appropriately, then with what exactly will your customers be engaging, and for what purpose?

Today's businesses need to stop running in place trying to keep up with the latest and greatest marketing tactics. Instead, their focus should be on developing those long-term strategies that build customer loyalty and convince prospects to buy. Yes, businesses need to be aware of new media and new approaches and be prepared to integrate them. But they need to do this in a way that makes sense for their business. They need to maintain a clear focus above the din of the roaring crowd—above the marketing noise.

If you're like most of us, you don't have the luxury of starting from a clean slate when you're developing marketing strategies. You likely have existing customers, existing channels and relationships, existing ways of doing business. With limited resources, you're not able to integrate every new tactic as it appears. You may not be sure how to prioritize all of these options.

I created the Dynamic Marketing Leverage assessment model as a way to capture the key elements critical to the success of serious marketing initiatives. Not every organization needs to invest equally in each leverage factor, but it's to your benefit to consciously consider where you will make marketing investments so that you can create the strategic marketing program your business needs to be successful and grow.

It's time to move the discussion away from today's latest hot marketing tools and tactics to what really counts: convincing customers to trust you with their business—not just once, but time and time again.

It's time to get above the noise.

I hope this book will start you on the path to that journey.

PART I

The Marketing Landscape

1

In the Heart of the Noise

I've spent my career in marketing, advising clients like Cisco Systems, NetApp, PayPal, Plantronics, Autodesk, Applied Materials, Sun Microsystems, and others on everything from branding to strategy to market analysis. I'm also a classical pianist. I'd like to start our discussion with a story about music that illustrates what can happen when you rise above the noise.

It was November 1923. Bandleader Paul Whiteman wanted to stage an experimental jazz concert in New York City the following February. He asked composer George Gershwin to create a concerto-like piece for the event. Gershwin declined, thinking he wouldn't have time to compose a piece of the complexity required.

Gershwin thought that was that. Then he saw an article in the *New York Tribune* in January 1924 noting that he, Gershwin, was at work on a jazz concerto for Whiteman's event. With only five weeks left, Gershwin scrambled to compose the piece. It was completed and orchestrated just eight days before the premiere.

According to historians, the program was quite long. It included twenty-six separate musical movements, plus a pre-concert lecture by Whiteman. Many of the pieces sounded similar. The ventilation system in the concert hall was broken. Gershwin's new composition was second to last on the program. By that time, many people in the audience were losing their patience. The room quieted. A haunting clarinet solo began, and American music was never the same.[1]

The new piece caught the attention of nearly everyone who heard it. Nearly a century later, *Rhapsody in Blue* is considered a cornerstone of our American musical heritage. Thousands of arrangements have been played in settings from musical salons to airports, and featured in genres from movies to TV commercials. United Airlines licensed the piece in the mid-1980s and is still using *Rhapsody* as its theme music three decades later.

Customers today sit in the equivalent of that hot, stuffy hall in New York. We are all overwhelmed with a seemingly endless parade of marketing messages from an ever-increasing variety of media. There's no break. No room to breathe. And it all sounds the same. As a businessperson, you need to understand how your marketing team can help your company stand out above the noise. You need to know how your organization can use marketing to create lasting business success and strategic advantage.

The idea for *Rhapsody in Blue* came to Gershwin on a train ride to Boston. He told his biographer Isaac Goldberg in 1931, "It was on the train, with its steely rhythms, its rattle-ty bang, that is so often so stimulating to a composer—I frequently hear music in the very heart of the noise..."[2]

What George Gershwin did in Aeolian Hall in New York City on February 12, 1924, was to get above the noise. This book addresses how you can use marketing to do the same for your business.

What Is Noise, Anyway?

The *Merriam-Webster Dictionary* defines noise in several ways, but the most relevant definitions are "any sound that is undesired or interferes with one's hearing of something" and "irrelevant or meaningless data or output occurring along with desired information."[3]

For senders, noise is what gets in the way of delivering their message. For the receivers, noise is what disturbs their sense of equilibrium, the normal pleasantness of their day. In business, noise is what prevents us from making appropriate connections with customers. It's what distracts us from maintaining focus. It's what prolongs the sales process, causes misunderstandings with customers, and leads to squandered opportunities.

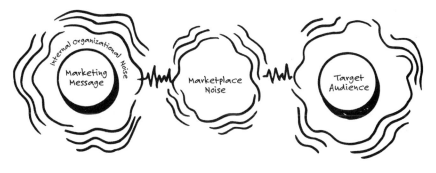

FIGURE 1-1: Noise

As marketers, we contend with two types of noise. The first is the noise in the marketplace. This may be from competitors, from unclear and unfocused messaging, or from a barrage of communications released simultaneously across a wide spectrum of channels. The second is the noise that builds within our own organizations. Even if you have great creative concepts, terrific messaging, and outstanding marketing campaigns, you'll still need to compete for resources and attention with all the other activities happening *within* your organization on a day-to-day basis.

Have your executives bought in to what your marketing team has proposed? Are you aligned with executive strategy, working together with the rest of the organization to fulfill the corporate vision? Do you have the support of your CIO when it comes to accessing the data you'll need to effectively target the right customers? Is your customer support team properly resourced to handle the aftermath of a successful marketing campaign?

One way to get above the noise factor is to simply try and be louder than everyone else. We all know people who try this. Their strategy when entering a large, loud conversation is to simply talk louder and LOUDER and **LOUDER** until they're shouting above the rest. This may work for a limited audience for a short period of time, but it's not sustainable, thank goodness!

A second way to defeat noise is with absolute silence. This may work for monks who have chosen a life of solitude and silence, but in the business world, silence will not help your business prosper. Within an organization, silence will not gain favor for the marketing organization among peers and colleagues clamoring for recognition and resources.

There's a third, more effective way to cut through the noise, and that's by creating a positive sound. A sound that people want to hear. A sound that makes people want to stop what they're doing and listen. A sound that resonates with your target audience. The music in the heart of the noise.

How does this work?

First, like Gershwin on the train to Boston, you'll need to become aware of the ambient noise around you. Understand what's going on in your environment. What are the dynamics of the market in which you intend to compete?

Second, you'll have to listen carefully to what your customers are saying: to what's working for them, what's frustrating them, where they need help, where they *don't* want you to interfere. Then, and only then, can you craft your response. Do it in a way that combines messages and media to create a powerful, pleasant sound, and the results will be music to your customers' ears.

Remember that what's considered noise and what's considered beautiful music are within the ear of the listener, not the musician. Igor Stravinsky's *Rite of Spring* was considered so revolutionary at its debut in 1913 that it actually incited riots in Paris. The hard rock anthems of my youth were nothing but noise to my parents. Rap and hip-hop are noise to a country music fan and vice versa.

Marketing Today Can Be Downright Scary

Late-night infomercials promise us the ability to get in great physical shape, look younger, improve our sex lives, and sharpen our minds... just by purchasing the products offered for that low, low price. If it is so easy to do these things, why aren't we all thin, muscular, highly attractive, and operating at peak performance levels?

It's tempting to be enticed by a magic pill or an exciting new device that offers a quick shortcut to the goal. Personally, I'd love to be able to sit down at the piano and play a Beethoven piano sonata immediately.

But I know it's not that simple. There's ongoing work required to get to an optimal level of performance. No magic pill changes that.

Just like anyone else, marketers can be distracted by the idea of the quick fix. We may be looking for a fast, easy way to achieve our objectives. We can also become enamored of technology, hoping it will allow us to circumvent the hard work and long processes previously required to be successful. The problem is, we need the basics of marketing—knowing our customer, building a solid product at an attractive price, promoting it in the right places—just like we need good habits and exercise. Without these, we will find ourselves on the wrong track, with badly performing marketing campaigns that leave us wondering where we went off key.

Marketing above the noise takes strategic thinking. It's not something you can throw together quickly and expect to revolutionize your business immediately. It takes time to understand the market, to get to know your customers and prospects, to learn about your competitors, and to become fully aware of the environment in which you sell.

On the other hand, some of the key factors are so timeless and basic that you may read this and say, gee, is that all there is? But just like learning to play an instrument, knowing what to do is the simple part. Exercising the discipline to do that right thing on an ongoing basis is what's tough.

If you follow my recommendations, you won't necessarily be on the bandwagon of the Next Biggest Coolest Thing. If being first to market is your chief goal, feel free to stop reading and jump into the fray. However, before you go, remember that Apple was not first to market with an MP3 player or a smartphone. Google was not the first online search engine, nor was Facebook the first social network.

Business success is not about being first. It's about building a sustainable competitive advantage by doing what's necessary to stand out from the crowd and get above the noise.

What Does Mastery Look Like?

How will you know when your organization is effectively getting above the noise? The answer will differ from company to company, but there are several indicators that your organization is succeeding.

To start, you're likely to see more definitive results from your marketing campaigns and initiatives. When you have solid metrics in place, it will be easier to see when an initiative is delivering and when it is not pulling its weight. If you know exactly what your strategy is, who your customers are, and what your marketplace is doing, you'll be able to assess whether your messages are resonating. But there are other less obvious benefits of marketing above the noise.

You'll find your organization is less reactive and less driven by "fire drills"—false emergencies that waste people's time. Interestingly, I've found that in many, many cases, the folks putting out the so-called fires are also the arsonists. Beware!

You'll see more thought leadership. Your marketing team will be looked to as thought leaders. This may occur at several levels—within your business or organization, within your industry, or in a more general business sense. Zappos, for example, is seen as a leader in customer service practices rather than in the sale of shoes, even though the company is extremely effective at that, too.

Marketing will be seen more as a driver, setting direction and driving strategy. This is opposed to just taking orders from a set of constituents with a seemingly endless appetite for ordering more, more, more marketing deliverables and wanting them now, now, now. In one organization I worked with, this situation was so bad, I threatened to buy the marketing leaders T-shirts with the inscription, "Would you like fries with that?"

Marketing will be part of the core business discussions. Too often, marketing is brought in to implement decisions that have already been made. After showing results from strategic initiatives, however, marketing will become part of the corporate strategy discussion and take their proper seat at the table.

There will be more buzz in the industry and beyond about what your organization is doing. Others will use your organization as an example of marketing done well. Your executives will be invited to share best practices with other organizations.

You'll see higher engagement and loyalty from customers. This will allow you to grow your share of wallet and keep acquisition costs low. Customers will be more willing to collaborate with you in creating winning products and powerful marketing campaigns.

The company will make greater progress in terms of establishing and building a brand. Your brand will help differentiate you in the marketplace, providing the impetus for customers to consistently choose you over the alternatives available to them.

You'll see more growth. This is real growth, above and beyond the rate of market or industry growth.

Finally, you'll make better use of scarce resources. Employees will be more engaged and enthusiastic. That, in turn, leads to less stress and more excitement in general. And what's the life of a marketer about, if not to have a little fun?

Who Does Strategic Marketing Effectively?

It's a funny thing. When I asked around for examples of companies that market above the noise, not many hands went up. It's much easier to find examples of companies that are *not* managing their marketing well (for example, those with the bad taste to try to inject humor into plane crashes, military coups, or natural disasters, and those that do a plain vanilla job). It's tough to find great examples.

In researching this book, I spoke with people at companies outside the typical business-to-consumer (B2C) space. In particular, I was interested in finding organizations that have really impacted their organizations by leveraging marketing well. For some companies, like Zillow (profiled in chapter 7), marketing helped create an entirely new category—in Zillow's case, that of online real estate marketplaces. Others, like Caribou

Coffee (chapter 4), have used effective marketing strategies to stand out in the crowded, competitive retail coffee market.

The examples spread through the book vary in terms of industry, audience, organization size, and maturity of both the company and the market they serve. One thing, however, is common. None of them had an extremely large marketing budget. In some cases, the resources allocated to marketing were quite small. In others, there was a reasonable budget but not an excessive one. The days of marketing organizations having carte blanche to spend whatever they deem necessary are way behind us, for better or for worse.

The organizations I've featured are creative and innovative. And they are resilient. When something didn't work, they picked themselves up, shrugged off the setback, and went on to try other avenues. I hope they will serve as examples to you, regardless of the industry or market you serve, and certainly without relevance to the dollars you have available to you for marketing.

How Do You Get Above the Noise?

First, it helps to understand the environment in which you play. A typical conversational voice sounds glaringly loud inside a quiet spa, but can't be heard at all in the midst of a rock concert. Similarly, a marketer needs to know when to shout and when to talk quietly yet convincingly to customers and prospects.

It also helps to understand where marketing is today and how we got here. It's true that some parts of marketing have changed dramatically in the last few years. You'll need to understand and integrate those new realities into your marketing mind-set to be successful. But, just as importantly, there are core marketing concepts that are timeless. They haven't changed in thousands of years and they won't likely change in the future. They provide the foundation that will allow you to better leverage new tools and technologies in the future.

Finally, you need to harmonize well with the rest of your organization. This is not a solo performance. It's a team effort. To succeed in the long run, you'll need to get to know your fellow players and understand how you can create powerful and pleasant sounds together.

The Dynamic Market Leverage Model

The Dynamic Market Leverage Model looks at eight marketing principles that have been at the core of good marketing initiatives for a long, long time. In fact, these eight principles are really timeless truths for marketing:

FIGURE 1-2: The Dynamic Market Leverage Model

- **Strategy**: We need to start with a business strategy that effectively anticipates customer, market, technology, and business needs.
- **Products**: We must have a good-quality product offering that meets customer needs better than the alternatives.
- **Customers**: We need to understand who our customers are, what they need, want, and desire, and how we can help them.
- **Brand**: We need to build a strong brand and reputation in the minds of our key audiences.
- **Communication**: We need to have a good way to communicate the value we provide.
- **Market analysis**: We need to understand the market environment in which we compete.

- **Operations**: We need to be able to deliver, track, and analyze our marketing activities.
- **Sales channels**: We need to work hand in hand with those who sell our product in order to be successful.

These factors help us focus in the marketplace, but too often we forget that marketers exist within organizations. Without the right internal momentum, marketing initiatives often get stuck in an internal rut and never see the light of day. So the Dynamic Market Leverage Model also looks at the five momentum factors that help propel an organization forward: **organizational commitment, resources, people, technology,** and **environment.** By reviewing both internal and external factors, the Dynamic Market Leverage tool will help you determine where you need to focus more marketing attention for your business.

We'll review each of these factors within the book and provide examples of how organizations have effectively cut through the noise to make an impact. Let's start by looking at how dramatically the marketing environment has changed in the last few years.

2

Today's Marketing Environment: The Tempo Accelerates

It was the hottest thing on the planet: a new technology that allowed users to interact in a way they'd never been able to do before, using the Internet to create a virtual community, connect with friends and colleagues, and share personal and professional information with like-minded individuals. Users staked out their own turf and invited others to join them. They created their own way of interacting with one another, their own language, even their own currency.

In 2007, the number of accounts registered for this new technology doubled to two million users within a single eight-week period. The excitement was tangible. This was the future, no doubt about it. Businesses and corporations began to line up to establish a presence on this platform of the future. This was where personal relationships would be developed, commerce transacted, brands promoted. The message was clear: if, as a marketer, you weren't there with a full marketing presence, you would undoubtedly be left behind.

Was this Facebook? Twitter? Myspace?

Not exactly. The once red-hot Second Life was founded within a few months of Facebook in 2003. But a decade later the bloom was off the rose. While Facebook had grown from 20 million to well over 1.1 billion unique users during this time, the number of active users for Second Life, had sputtered to only about 550,000.[1] That's a funny thing about hot technologies—they arrive with fanfare and next thing you know, everyone's on the bandwagon. This is the biggest thing since sliced bread, you're told. You'll be left behind if you don't join the party.

That may be true, or it may not. How can you predict which of these innovations will take off? How do you know when to jump so as not to miss the boat? Is it wise to wait and see whether the latest offering will achieve anything near what's promised? The buzz one might gain by being seen as an early adopter of the latest hot marketing platform is often outweighed by the cost to ramp up support for such a new technology—especially if it appears your customers and prospects haven't flocked in droves to get on board, as initially projected. Let's look at the challenges we face in today's marketing environment.

What Happened to the World As We Knew It?

I've lived and worked in the heart of Silicon Valley for the past twenty years. But being at the center (literally and figuratively) of many of the technologies that have transformed our society over the last two decades didn't necessarily put the Valley at the forefront of marketing innovation.

Silicon Valley has a special kind of excitement. It's a fast-paced, exhilarating ride, where start-ups and venture capitalists connect over breakfast and megadeals are consummated over drinks in the evening (not to mention products and strategies hatched over lunch). When you lived here, you always believed you were doing something to change the world—and, more often than not, you were right.

Silicon Valley has always been driven by technology—whether it was oscillators and semiconductors, networking and personal computers, or mobile and social media. We followed the *Field of Dreams* mantra: "If you build it, they will come." And for decades that was true, most of the time. What is also true is that marketing has not been a highly prized skill for much of the Valley's history. Technology sold products. Marketing came afterward and facilitated the process, sometimes. The traditional marketing gospel familiar to consumer packaged goods companies was practically unheard of and very rarely adopted among companies in the Valley.

Fast-forward to today, and we find an interesting situation. New technology—in the shape of online delivery of content (including music, books, and other applications), user-generated content, and interactive social media tools—has changed what we refer to as marketing. It's not just about the technology, but what the technology lets us *do* in terms of creating new products, interacting with customers, responding to customer needs, developing new delivery mechanisms, and so on.

The pace of new techniques and technologies continues to pick up, moving faster and faster, as if someone turned up the speed on the marketing merry-go-round. Just like a kid in a candy store, businesses want to taste each and every possible new concoction. They all look and sound so good!

The funny thing, though, about riding this merry-go-round, is that you can get pretty darn dizzy. Dizzy enough so that if you can't find a way to steady yourself, you'll make yourself quite sick. You then may be forced to jump off the ride and miss the innovations that are really important.

Your competitors are at the same carnival. If they've figured out how to stay focused, they can move ahead of you while you take time to catch your breath, regain your footing, and wonder just what went wrong. If they've chosen judiciously from the marketing options available, they'll be feeling satisfied and full. Meanwhile, you're madly looking for the right tonic to handle the aftermath of an appetite run wild.

The question is, how can you balance the need to stay competitive and up-to-date while restraining the urge to jump in and try all the new marketing tactics at once? Because there's another truth about Silicon Valley: for all the successful companies launched, there are hundreds and hundreds of organizations like Second Life that don't live up to expectations. This happens even though at the time they had what seemed like incredible technologies and a couldn't-miss opportunity.

Change Is the New Constant

When I lived in Boston many years ago, people used to tell me, "If you don't like the weather, wait a minute, it will change." That's been the situation in business over the last few years. Everything is changing: technology, the economy, the business environment, and even people themselves. So much is in flux; it's hard to keep track of what's current at any given time.

Technology adoption continues at a faster and faster pace. According to the popular Web video "Did You Know 2013,"[2] it took thirty-eight years for radio to hit fifty million users, thirteen years for television to break that threshold, four years for the Internet, three years for iPods, and only two years for Facebook. By late 2012, 72 percent of Apple's revenue came from iPhones and iPads, with one hundred million iPads sold since the product's launch two and a half years earlier.[3] By mid-2014, that number had doubled again to two hundred million.[4] And, in September 2014, Apple sold ten million of its brand new iPhone6 and 6 Plus phones *the first weekend* they were available.[5]

Feeling overwhelmed yet? More than 160 *billion* e-mails are sent daily—97 percent of which are spam.[6] Add to that the 58 million tweets sent per day,[7] the hundred billion Google searches each month,[8] and the quarter million Instagram photos shared per second.[9] *Per second.* That's 21.6 *billion* pictures posted online every single day. No wonder we're having trouble standing out from the noise.

People are changing, too. For one thing, demographics are shifting dramatically. By the start of this decade, members of generation Y—the millennials (born between the 1980s and the early 2000s) outnumbered baby boomers. That means an increasingly large portion of society has grown up with not just the Internet, smartphones, and other digital technologies, but in a world where the war against terrorism supplanted the Cold War. Organics are found at Walmart and not just at Whole Foods, and many people really don't know where their appliances, cars, or clothing were really manufactured.

In 2012, according to a Nielsen report, for the first time, more albums were sold in digital music stores than any other location.[10] But by mid-2014, even digital downloads were declining. U.S. listeners streamed 70.3 billion songs in the first half of that year—an increase of 42 percent over the first half of 2013.[11]

Probably the biggest change of all, though, is the change that's going on in the hearts and minds of our prospects and customers: a change *in expectations*. In an era of always-on, real-time communication, our audiences now expect us to act quickly and respond in real time to their needs.

In her book *The 24-Hour Customer: New Rules for Winning in a Time-Starved, Always-Connected Economy*, strategist Adrian Ott discusses how our relationship to time in general has changed in today's world. TiVo and DVRs taught us to time shift to watch entertainment. Games on mobile devices allow us to time slice (divide a task into very small, easily digestible segments). Customers make decisions based on convenience, value, and habit, as well as motivation. Yet in spite of all the technology available to them, they still feel overwhelmed, overworked, and overstressed.

More and more, customers want us to anticipate what they'll need in the future, and adapt accordingly. They expect that, based on conversations with us about our products and services, we will change what we provide to them and the way we provide it.

FIGURE 2-1: Today's Environment

Here's the catch, though. Customers may want all of these new things, but they aren't willing to give up what they've been getting from their favorite products and services all these years. They want at least the same level of quality, the same value for the price, and the support systems to which they've become accustomed. They don't want us to stop doing the old things because we're now doing others. They want to have a vested interest in creating and driving brands. But they want us to continue providing the brands they know and love. In many ways, they want to have their cake and eat it too.

Tools like Twitter and Facebook provide consumers with the ability to comment on products and brands in near real time. If only businesses and brands would take the time to listen to what they're saying! But what does this feedback mean? Do the comments you're gathering through the Twitter stream represent the overall pulse of key customers? Or do they represent the views of a few dissenting individuals? Do they presage early trends that need to be followed closely?

Today, change happens faster and more dramatically than ever, and it happens on a continuous basis. Those of us in business need to be prepared to move quickly and decisively while not walking away from what got us here in the first place. And therein lies the rub.

Do I Stay or Do I Go?

One of the challenges of today's environment is that there is no time to stop and wait for things to calm down or solidify. Almost as soon as one change is implemented, along comes another that requires our attention—sometimes obsoleting what we've just adopted.

The media upon which we've depended for the past several decades are devolving right before our eyes. Print newspapers and magazines are shrinking and disappearing by the dozen. Network television has lost its stranglehold on the advertising market. In their place we find not only Web-based versions of our favorite publications or TV shows but new formats and delivery vehicles, from blogs and YouTube videos to mobile phones and tablets. In 2013, for the first time, Internet advertising spending (including search, display, and paid content) exceeded broadcast television spending,[12] and in 2014 digital networks held their first "upfront" media buying event, similar to those held for television.

It's not just traditionally produced and distributed content being made available through streaming services. Netflix has created critically acclaimed original content like *House of Cards* and *Orange Is the New Black*, solidifying the phenomenon of "binge watching." Amazon jumped into the fray too, releasing six new original shows in 2014, in addition to its political comedy *Alpha House*.

Speaking of Amazon, today its most popular product line is not physical books or music or software, but e-books sold for the Kindle e-book reader or the Kindle app for other mobile devices. The implications are huge, and not just for authors and publishers: as marketers, how do we reach an audience that consumes what used to be printed material on an electronic reader? Who controls access to the customer? How does a company or product differentiate itself in this new world? And what happens when the Kindle, or Barnes & Noble's e-reader, the Nook, are quickly obsoleted by newer devices? How do we build effective marketing strategies in this rapidly evolving world?

Should we keep using the tried-and-true strategies, which may not be as effective as they once were? Or should we implement new strategies and tactics that may be not just unproven but also costly in terms of the time and effort required? Will these new hot marketing tools yield the results we're expecting? Will these techniques be as effective as our previous marketing efforts? Or should we perhaps integrate some old and new methods?

The problem is that too many organizations try everything at once. They follow the axiom that if some of a given thing is good, more of it is better. Consumers, the recipients of this barrage, feel as if they're being hit from all angles. No wonder our target audiences have donned the proverbial noise-canceling headphones in search of a little solitude amid the cacophony.

Nobody Goes There Anymore—It's Too Crowded

A funny thing happened on the way back from the recent recession. A lot of organizations got religion about marketing. In good times, it's easy to attract customers. There's plenty of money to go around and success breeds more success. In a tight economy, with fewer dollars spent, the need to capture as many new customers as possible and hold on to existing ones becomes imperative.

Some companies become shortsighted and cut back on marketing programs and initiatives in an attempt to shave expenses and balance budgets. But many others see that marketing is an investment that helps set the stage for their continued success. And still others begin to realize their own momentum and good looks aren't enough to carry them forward to meet their revenue and profitability goals. The result is more and more marketing noise generated on a daily basis.

Think of this as a game of reverse musical chairs. Each company has a set of chairs, and prospects and customers scurry around, deciding where to land. However, instead of one chair being removed each round, the number of chairs increases on a regular basis—with more options being added all the time. Those whose chairs aren't occupied can't afford to stay in the game very long. As the owner of one of the chairs, you have to do your darnedest to make prospects choose your chair rather than the alternatives. You have to show prospects that you have the right features and benefits, the right value at the right time. You'll also need to reassure the people who've been comfortably situated with you for years that they want to remain seated where they are.

As this process unfolds, life gets more complicated. More activity and noise are added to an already loud and complicated system. It's a system where everyone is talking at once, all the time, using every medium possible, following us to places we didn't even know they could go.

The problem is not a lack of options but an abundance of wealth. We have *too many* marketing activities—they're coming out of our ears. The good news is very few people have learned how to play the game effectively. That's why it becomes even more important for you, as a marketer, to understand which resources you need to develop so you can execute the most effective strategy possible for your organization. You'll need to tailor your plan for the products and services you offer, the customers you serve, and the environment in which you compete.

Does Any of This Marketing Stuff Really Work?

We marketers want to take part in the fun of Facebook, the timeliness of Twitter, the excitement of YouTube. We want to be mobile. We want to be social. But how do we know whether or not any of these tactics are relevant to our business?

In every market there are early adopters who will grab every innovation and jump at each opportunity to try something new and creative. However, the fact that we have early adopters means, by definition, that the bulk of users are *not* moving as quickly. Look at the context in which your customers are using a new medium or technology. Is it in their personal life, their business life, across all their interactions, or just during a small part of their day? By 2013, Facebook already had well over a billion users. At first glance, that means it's likely many of your customers or prospects have accounts on Facebook, one of the world's most popular destination sites.

However, depending on your business, not all of these people (and perhaps just a small subgroup of them) are using their Facebook accounts *in the context of your business.* If you have a B2C or consumer-oriented business, your customers are likely to be interacting with you on Facebook. But if your organization is business-to-business (B2B) focused, this is less likely to be the case. So while we see hundreds of thousands of fans of Starbucks or In-N-Out Burger or Best Buy, it's much less likely that customers of medical-testing products or industrial components or legal services are going to publicly identify themselves on Facebook as "liking" these particular organizations. That's not the context in which these customers see Facebook. Will they eventually use it for B2B interaction? Perhaps. Should we push them forward now? The answer is, it depends. It's still not clear that Facebook is where many business-to-business customers go today to create or join a community.

Not every product or service lends itself to every marketing medium. What's important is not to be on the front lines of the revolution, but to be where your customers are now and where you reasonably believe they're headed. Sometimes that will be on the bleeding edge. More often, it's not.

Help! I'm Already Dizzy!

There's plenty of information available in near real time about all of the new tactics, technologies, and approaches to branding and marketing available to us. But with all the attention to these details, as we spin faster and faster around the merry-go-round, we're losing the big picture. We need to focus on how organizations should actually use marketing to create and grow profitable, successful businesses.

Until you've stopped to understand the fundamental facts about your market, your customers, and the environment in which you compete, all that frenzied activity is wasteful and maybe even dangerous. In fact, it's likely driving your customers and prospects quite mad. Rather than add more and more to the mix, stop what you are doing. Right this minute.

Breathe. Take time to consider the concepts and case studies that are outlined in this book so you can stand out above the noise, with a strategy that will grow your business effectively and profitably.

3

What Hasn't Changed:
Timeless Marketing Truths

We hear so much about how marketing has changed dramatically over the past few years. In some ways it has. We have user-generated content, one-to-one customizable marketing, social media, online communities, mobile technology, and so on. But in some ways, marketing hasn't changed a bit in the last ten thousand years or so.

Let's travel back to a time before the Internet, before the Industrial Revolution, even before the advent of written communications. People lived off the land—farming, hunting, fishing. They ate what they grew or shepherded, made their own clothes, fashioned their own weapons. In good years, there was an abundance of whatever a farmer was raising. In bad years, there was not enough to properly feed and clothe a family.

Eventually, we humans realized we could swap goods: if my chickens were particularly fruitful and laid extra eggs, and your cows were particularly productive, giving additional milk, and the farmer down the road had extra wheat or rice...we could all come together and help each other out. As word spread that such exchanges were occurring, more and more local people showed up with different offerings to add to the mix. This regular barter or exchange of goods became known as a *market*, and it had many of the same characteristics of the markets we see today.

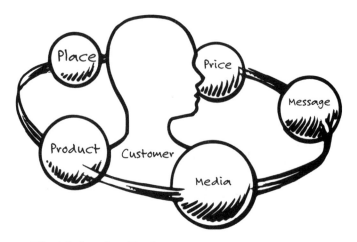

FIGURE 3-1: The Marketplace Environment

To start with, each producer had to have a quality **product**. If my eggs were not fresh or your cheese was not tasty, neither of us was going to last very long in the arrangement. We had to show up at the right **place** at the right time...if everyone else was meeting Thursday at noon, and I showed up Friday morning instead, I would have no one with whom to trade, and I'd go home with the same wares I'd brought with me.

We had to understand who our **customers** were and we had to package our offerings accordingly. How many eggs would a family likely need in a week? Would people who needed dairy products likely be more interested in milk, butter, or cheese? Without refrigeration, how much milk could they feasibly use in a week—a cup, a quart, or a gallon?

We needed to have the right **price** for our potential customers. Would anyone really believe one container of butter was worth three dozen eggs? On the other hand, the savvy farmer would soon learn that she could command a high price for the finest aged cheese in the land.

We needed the right **message** in promoting our product: Was your wool softer than anyone else's? Would it keep buyers warmer through the cold winter, or was it simply less expensive? Would the buyer look more attractive than other villagers when wearing garments made with this wool?

We needed to let others know what we had to offer. This started with word of mouth at the market (and yes, there was word of mouth, before we called it social media!). It extended to more traditional marketing, advertising and promoting the offerings available in shops and town squares, using what would eventually be known as **media** as time went on. We may no longer drag our goods to a physical marketplace (though there's been a resurgence of farmer's markets lately as part of the move to more local, fresher, organic produce). But all of the factors that were key for our ancestors are still relevant today: **product, price, customers, message, media.** The vehicles we use to reach our customers have changed but the theory behind the practice of marketing is still rooted in that village square experience of centuries ago.

Marketing Doesn't Make You Do It

One of the most frustrating myths that marketers face is the idea that marketing can create need or force people to buy things they don't need or that they've decided they don't want. Let me share a secret: marketers *do not* have the power to make this happen…and if we did have some magic that compelled people to buy, it would be highly unethical to use it.

Good marketing *can*, however, make the difference in whether people are convinced to part with their money, or whether they keep waiting and watching for something better to come along. Marketing can persuade a prospect to go with Company A rather than Company B— because the messages resonate more strongly, because the prospect feels more comfortable or secure with that option, or because the prospect has been made aware of a need or want he wasn't focused on before. Or, the potential customer may simply feel compelled to purchase because of her affinity for one company or the other's brand. Marketing *does* create and build brands.

What marketing *can't* do is put a figurative gun to people's heads and convince them to buy something they have already decided they don't want or need. There's no magic spell that puts people into a marketing trance and forces them to sign up for products or services they aren't interested in or that aren't relevant to them. Even those late-night infomercials tap into the unmet needs of their insomniac audience.

Now, as a consumer, you may find yourself intrigued by the marketing message of a product that doesn't fit your self-imposed ideas about what's right for your needs. That's not because of an insidious plot to introduce new ideas into your head. More likely it's because you had an unmet, unarticulated need, and an astute marketer tapped into it.

Health and beauty purveyors tap into our desire to be in better shape and look younger or sexier—but if I despise cold-weather sports, no amount of marketing will convince me to invest in a vacation to a ski resort. Conversely, although I may not be consciously thinking about a ski trip, if a marketer taps into my key beliefs and unmet needs (whether I'm actively looking for a vacation or not), a trip to the snow country might become something I decide to pursue.

Good marketing meshes with the needs and wants your customers and prospects most likely already have. The key is understanding what your potential customers are trying to tell you, even if they can't articulate it clearly themselves. As we'll discuss later in the book, it's all about them, not you.

The Foundation Is Still the Foundation

Not many people start building a house by choosing the window treatments or floor coverings first, yet that's what often happens in marketing. Consider the process of building a new house. You need a site and a builder, but even before that, you need to know what kind of house you want. How many people will likely live there? Will it be on the water or will it have a mountain view? How much of the land will be taken up by the house versus a yard or other exterior features? From here you can start to design the house of your dreams. You'll consider how big the living area should be, how many bedrooms you'd like, whether the house will have one floor or two, and so on.

Some of these wants are critical, while others are just nice-to-haves. You may want a gorgeous view, but if you've got kids, choosing a location with better schools may trump the scenery. Once you've got the design, your construction team will start by building a foundation, ensuring that the core of your building is solid and can support the weight of what will be built on top. When the project is complete, the quality of the finishes will be evident. But the building works because the framework underneath—the part you don't see—was built correctly.

The same thing happens with marketing. Marketing is not a monolithic process. It involves multiple steps. Marketers who rise above the noise have discrete strategies and tactics that they use at each step. You'll first need to understand what you'd like to build. Setting strategy first will give you a strong foundation.

Then you'll need to understand your audience and what motivates them. The type of marketing that's appropriate for an organization depends on who your prospective customers are and where they are in the purchase process.

The Five Stages of the Purchase Process

The purchase process is a spectrum that starts when you enter a market and target specific prospects. It's logical to think that getting a prospect to purchase is your aim. However, purchase by itself is not the goal if you want to build a sustainable business.

FIGURE 3-2: The Five-Stage Purchase Process

The process starts with **awareness.** Just like the dairy farmer and shepherd of yore, your prospective customers need to know that you exist and that you have a product or service that may fit their needs. If they don't know about you, they can't buy from you. It sounds simple, but I can't tell you how many times I've talked to companies that want to skip over this phase completely.

Any seasoned sales rep will tell you he's been in the situation where, in the midst of a sales call, a prospect says, "Gee, what you have is a great fit for us. If only I'd known about this last week, before I made the decision to go with someone else!" Whoops. Marketing to build awareness focuses on telling prospects who you are, what you stand for, and what they can expect from you.

In 2013, Manheim Automotive merged its used car dealer financing operation, Manheim Auto Financial Services, with an innovative start-up operation in the same field called Dealer Services Corp (DSC). The new organization, rebranded NextGear Capital, brought thousands of customers from both predecessors into the fold, creating a commanding presence in the market for wholesale used car dealership financing, or floor planning.

But no one knew who this new entity was, which is why NextGear's initial marketing efforts were focused solely around awareness and brand building. Once the target market began recognizing the NextGear brand and name, then the company could move to other marketing objectives, including building market share and getting a higher share of wallet from existing customers.

Once you've made the prospect aware of what you're offering, you need to move her along the path to **consideration.** Just because a prospect is aware of what you offer, it doesn't mean she is going to *consider* your product or service for her own needs.

Living in the Bay Area, I am very much aware of Tesla all-electric cars, designed and built locally. Tesla has done an outstanding job of building brand awareness. The company is in the news on a regular basis, and its cars are considered symbols of success for the Silicon Valley set. As a result, I see hundreds of Tesla Model S sedans on local streets and freeways.

However, when I purchased my most recent vehicle I knew that I needed a crossover/SUV that would fit my Siberian husky easily in the back, and I wanted to be able to drive 300-plus miles on a tank of gas.

Tesla's $80,000 sedan that needs to be charged every 150 miles was not a vehicle I actively *considered* during my search.

That's why it's so important to understand your customers and what it is that's important to them. We'll delve more deeply into customer needs in chapter 5.

Getting a prospect to make an initial **purchase** is actually the middle of the process. There are very few things, bought by either consumers or businesses, that are once-in-a-lifetime purchases. Customers usually purchase items on a pilot or trial basis. Even commercial airliners, which cost hundreds of millions of dollars, are usually purchased as options. The airline reserves the right to buy one or more planes, but can cancel (at a cost) if its needs change or if the manufacturer can't meet delivery time frames.

When marketing at the initial purchase phase, the goal is to reach prospects and help them overcome reluctance to buy. Try-and-buy offers are a common tactic, and they're effective. Many online services offer a free trial period or use a "freemium" model, where the basic service is free but there's a charge for the full-fledged offering. However, they'll also capture a user's payment information to ease the process of upgrading to the paid service. We'll discuss this in more detail in chapter 7.

Think this only applies to small-ticket items? What's the first thing a car salesperson does when you start eying a model in the showroom? She'll hand you the keys and have you take that new car out for a test drive.

Once a customer has purchased your offering initially, you want to move him to **preference.** In this phase, with all else being equal, a customer will prefer your offering over other options. Preferences form because we establish habits and behaviors. We develop a taste for a brand of soft drink or fast food or clothing, so we automatically gravitate toward that brand without thinking much about it. In some cases—consumer banking, for example—preference is built because it's much easier to maintain the status quo than to make changes that may be only marginally better but require extra effort on our part.

Preference is a move in the right direction for marketers, but it can be easily overridden. For example, many soda drinkers have a strong preference for either Coke or Pepsi. If two vending machines are standing side by side, Coke drinkers will normally choose to buy from the Coke machine and the Pepsi lovers will choose Pepsi. But consider this: it's a hot summer day, you've been out in the heat building up a thirst, and you walk into an establishment that only sells Pepsi. Even those with a strong preference for Coke will likely break down and take the other brand of soft drink offered.

As another example, it's not easy to change banks. You'll need a new ATM card and you'll have to change your auto deposits and online payments. But consumers will make the switch if their existing bank is not treating them well (charging too many extra fees, perhaps). They'll also make a change if a dramatically better offer comes along (such as Square for credit card processing).

That's why the long-term goal of a marketing program is to build **loyalty.** Loyal customers have developed such a strong affinity for your offering and your brand that they will turn down alternatives that may be closer, cheaper, or more easily accessible. In some cases, loyal customers will actively evangelize *for* your brand or company.

A great example of a company with a loyal following is, of course, Apple. For years, I made a standing offer in my marketing classes to trade Mac users a brand-new PC of their choice for their existing Mac laptop. It was a safe bet. No one ever took me up on it. In fact, most of the time at least one person would take me to task for even making the offer. They made impassioned arguments about why Apple was so much better and even implied that I was ignorant for not already knowing that.

Loyal customers are less expensive to service, less price sensitive, and less likely to be influenced by competitive moves. Marketing to this group is about reinforcing what they already know and love about your offerings and your brand. It's making them feel there's no reason to go anywhere else with their business.

At any given time, your business may be focused on customers in multiple parts of the purchase process. An effective marketing team keeps this in mind when planning which marketing initiatives to implement, and, just as importantly, which initiatives *not* to undertake.

Climbing the Wrong Mountain

Moving forward with a marketing program without taking the time to outline a solid strategy is like going mountain climbing without understanding which mountain it is you're going to scale.

Imagine this. A friend goes to an outdoor store like REI and outfits herself at considerable expense with all the best climbing gear: clothing, equipment, supplies, etc. She looks good and feels good as she sets off to climb the first peak she sees. Let's presume for now that our friend is in good physical condition and able to undertake this kind of expedition. Off she goes up the mountain. The problem is that the higher she gets, the more she can see the bigger landscape. Partway up, she realizes that this is *not* the mountain she wanted to climb. She really wants to be on the mountain two peaks over.

She can't just jump from peak to peak. Instead, she'll need to come all the way back down, travel over to the other mountain, and start all over again. By this time, she's likely tired, hungry, and frustrated, and she's used up many of her supplies. The second climb will be much more difficult than the first.

Even worse, what if, as she climbs the first mountain, our friend looks out and realizes she really should be deep sea diving instead. Not only does she need to get down off the mountain and to the water, but she's also invested in all the wrong equipment.

I see similar scenarios unfold on a regular basis when marketing initiatives are implemented without considering the overarching strategy. Companies rush to get out "on the mountain" as quickly as possible. They spend a reasonable amount of time and money looking good as they start their trek. But, shortly, they realize they haven't targeted the correct customers. Their message isn't resonating with their key audience. Or the competitive situation has changed so that the mountain has "moved" and isn't nearly as attractive as they originally thought.

This wastes millions of dollars. Even more importantly, it squanders time, resources, and energy. While an organization is off climbing the wrong mountain, consumers have moved on or competitors have stepped in. There isn't always the time or resources available to go back for a mulligan.

Dynamic Market Leverage Factor 1: Strategy

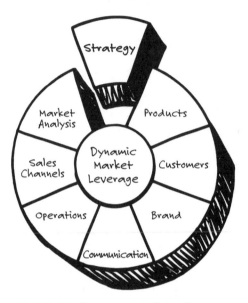

FIGURE 3-3: Dynamic Market Leverage Model—Strategy

Strategy is at the core of a solid marketing program. That's why it's the first of the eight key market leverage factors. Once you've decided you really do want to climb that mountain, strategy helps you determine where you need to focus to ensure a successful ascent. Do you want to generate awareness for a new product or a new category of products? That's a very different strategic focus than trying to increase share of wallet with a set of existing customers.

It's important to be clear about where you want to go and the reasons you want to get there. Developing an effective marketing strategy doesn't happen in a vacuum. It's impossible to build a successful strategy without understanding the vision and goals of the overall organization. Is the corporate focus on growth in terms of revenue or new customers? Is the business looking at maintaining or growing its business in existing markets, or expanding into new markets? Is the focus on customer acquisition or on improving margins?

Knowing these things, as a marketing leader, you can develop marketing goals that align closely with the organization's business goals and objectives. But that alone is not enough for a marketing strategy.

Successful marketing leaders build a clear vision and focus for the function. They then communicate this vision throughout both the marketing team and the bigger organization. Traditionally, marketing has been seen as the group responsible for implementation. It's the marketing team that creates advertising, generates promotions, builds the Website, and assembles the trade show booth for each show and event.

Execution is important. But being known as the greatest executors in the company should not be the marketing team's top goal. An effective strategic marketing organization will show leadership in developing and driving initiatives that will really impact the business. It's not just about delivering creative materials and events. A strategic marketing organization focuses on the *value* that marketing provides to the rest of the organization. Plans and initiatives are actionable and measurable. Innovation is encouraged.

Today, we have the tools to measure the impact of many, but not all, marketing initiatives. Not all metrics are created equal, as we'll discuss later. From a strategic standpoint, it's important to keep an eye on those metrics that really move the needle from a business perspective. Focus on those that are customer- and revenue-centric, rather than measuring inputs or internal engagement. Look at changes in market share, share of wallet, revenue, profits, or time to market—*not* the number of clicks or likes or follows.

What makes a strategic marketing organization stand out above the noise? How do you know when your organization is really working effectively? To start, you'll know when marketing leaders are called in to offer strategic input to other functions in the organization. You'll know when you see the organization look to marketing for guidance and direction, not just execution. You'll see other parts of the organization, from executives down to individual contributors, point to what marketing does and why it's so important to the ongoing success of the company.

If your organization isn't there yet, don't despair. This is an ongoing process, a journey. The leverage factors covered in this book will get you moving in the right direction.

4

What *Has* Changed:
The New Realities

While some aspects of marketing are timeless, those pieces that *have* changed over the last few years have transformed the marketing equation. This is not your grandfather's marketing world any more. In fact, it's not even your older brother's marketing world.

There are several areas that are dramatically and drastically different today than they were even a few years ago. There's a new approach to delivery, data, demand generation, and drivers. There's also a focus on conversations, content, and communities. In addition, there's a new paradigm for looking at media channels, based on these new realities. Let's look at each of these.

Delivery

The techniques and tools now available to deliver a product or service to market would be beyond the comprehension of Don Draper and his 1960s-era *Mad Men* colleagues. These range from the technology that allows rapid prototyping (and, with 3D printers, actual production of physical items) to the ability to develop and deliver a customized product or service offering geared to a specific set of customers.

Take XOAB as an example. XOAB (pronounced zo-ab), a start-up founded by brothers Rick and Neil Levine, designs, produces, and distributes high-end men's designer socks. That's right, designer socks—in a variety of vibrant geometric patterns and colors. These unique socks are designed, sourced, and manufactured in the United States in limited editions.

XOAB set out to solve the dilemma of why there were no interesting, complex-patterned socks that stretched to properly fit men's feet. It turns out that it's because the folks designing socks are far removed from the people who actually make them. As a result, patterns are designed in somewhat of a vacuum and they don't work well with automated knitting machines. Rick and Neil Levine created specialized software that generates pattern files that are downloaded directly into knitting machines to create socks that look great and fit comfortably, too.

XOAB's initial funding came from a Kickstarter campaign that allowed funders to choose socks from a set of initial limited designs in exchange for their support. The Levines, whose prior experience includes graphic design and engineering, as well as running an organic chocolate manufacturer, did their homework on textile manufacturing. They were told to do capacity planning based on a bell curve that presumed most customers would choose conservative colors and simple geometric patterns.

But that's not what happened.

Given the opportunity to choose whatever they wanted, people picked just about every possible combination. The breakdown of initial sock orders was all over the map. Instead of a bell curve, XOAB saw a completely flat distribution—the epitome of the long tail. Add in the choice of cotton or wool and two sizes, and it took more than 360 SKUs for XOAB to fulfill the initial Kickstarter orders alone.

The good news is that XOAB's business model allows for flexible and customizable delivery. In fact, XOAB became the first manufacturer to develop a method of stitching a unique bar code into each and every sock. This allows the company to trace the progress of each sock, to associate socks with customers (tracking taste and buying patterns), and even to associate certain socks and certain customers with the corresponding retailers that first introduced them to the product. This offers all kinds of interesting marketing opportunities for XOAB and its sales partners in the future.

If XOAB can change the way an everyday product like socks is delivered to market, imagine what these new delivery methods can do for other, more complex products. The implications for the way marketers approach product marketing are huge. If you haven't thought how these new technologies will impact your industry, you may be behind your competitors. Don Draper would be trembling in his boring black mid-ankle socks at the possibilities.

The Peripatetic Piano Teacher Comes to Her Students

For the past thirty-five years, the van der Linde family has opened their home and their lives to those who want to immerse themselves in the study of piano music. In 1969, Rosamond and Rein van der Linde couldn't find a summer piano camp for their children, so they decided to start their own. They filled a large mansion in Bennington, Vermont, with pianos (using every room, including the linen closet and the laundry) and called their program Summer Sonatina. Word spread and the camp caught on. It wasn't long before parents of campers were asking for a program of their own, and the adult Sonatas program was born in 1979.

The van der Linde's eldest daughter, Polly, has been immersed in music her entire life—as a performer, a teacher, and a counselor at her parents' camp. In 1991, Juilliard-educated Polly began managing Sonatina Enterprises; she and her husband, Dale, bought the business in 1998. Through the years, she's expanded the program to include a yearlong schedule of ten-day Sonata programs, as well as several five-day Intermezzo (short interlude) sessions. Pianists of all levels travel from as far away as Japan and New Zealand to participate in the programs, which include private instruction, master classes, lots and lots of practice time, and three meals a day prepared by a gourmet chef.

Polly van der Linde is a rare breed—a fun-loving and passionate musician and teacher with the ability to effectively teach the full spectrum of pianists, from highly accomplished lifelong performers to rank beginners sitting at a keyboard for the first time. For many years, she traveled around the country offering lessons and master classes to groups of Sonata participants eager for another taste of the Sonata experience between visits to Vermont. However, as family demands grew, it became harder and harder for Polly to take the show on the road.

Her solution: use technology to bring students closer to the Sonata experience. She and her IT/tech manager, Matt Moon, set up high-definition Webcams and microphones around her Steinway piano, so that master classes from Sonata could be live streamed to a worldwide audience over the Web. That helped, but students still wanted more. "How can we clone you?" they asked.

In the summer of 2014, a student who was moving to Vienna, Austria, wanted to find a way to continue his piano studies long distance. Polly responded with a new program: online piano lessons. Offered to pianists of all ages and skill levels, the lessons are conducted over Skype using the high-definition Webcams and microphones already in place. The four cameras let students see their teacher's face, as well as her hands from above and the side, and the musical score.

Each student sends Polly his repertoire in advance, so she can prepare and note particular passages to review. The only equipment required of the student (in addition to a piano!) is an iPod or laptop with Skype.

Delivering a new service to her existing market is fun, says Polly. "There's a new dynamic to the lesson. I get to see people in their own environment—sitting at the bench at their own piano. Students are more relaxed because they feel more at home. Because we've checked the setup in advance, we can focus 100 percent on the music."

Polly doubts online piano lessons will ever totally replace the in-person experience. But for those who'd like occasional coaching or specific help with a particular piece, there's now a way to provide it—with a lot less wear and tear on the piano teacher. That's the power of new delivery mechanisms in today's world.

Data

"Big Data" has become the fashionable term in the technology industry: if you're not capturing, analyzing, and acting on Big Data, you're not in the in crowd. Analyst firm Gartner defines Big Data as "high volume, high velocity, and/or high variety information assets that require new forms of processing to enable enhanced decision making, insight discovery and process optimization."[1]

Consumers are using Big Data to do everything from monitoring their exercise and diet (with tools like the Nike+ FuelBand and Fitbit fitness trackers) to comparing travel options, tracking prices, and finding coupons, and even accessing information in U.S. government databases, through a site called Data.gov.[2]

Businesses are using Big Data to interact with consumers. For example, in the health-care space alone, users can post personal health data and share interpretations with Curious, Inc.'s online forum. A second company, Ginger.io, collects health data via smartphone surveys. This data is shared with an individual's doctors, who can then suggest interventions at an early stage. Want to donate directly to patients in the developing world seeking medical treatment? A third start-up, Watsi, is a crowdfunding platform that allows users to do exactly that.[3]

But it's not just "Big" data that's revolutionized marketing. It's data of all sizes, shapes, and complexities. Many organizations are still just getting their hands around what might be called "Small Data." They're now starting to think about how to leverage basic point-of-sale (POS) information. They're also considering what to do with a better understanding of their customers and the products they've purchased in the past.

Take as an example Dave Martin, vice president of marketing and content for the Electronic Retailing Association (ERA). ERA is the trade association for direct response marketers, representing more than 450 companies and 3,500 individuals in that industry. As a small association, ERA doesn't have either the budget or the manpower to do all the marketing Martin would like to recruit new members and retain the ones the association currently has. So he has to be judicious in the way he spends money.

Martin hasn't yet been able to implement the latest marketing automation technology. He's had to be creative in working with his current e-mail marketing provider to customize e-mail blasts based on recipients' member status as well as their current purchases. A nonmember might receive a special conference offer. A member who has registered for a conference might receive an offer to upgrade to a more comprehensive option.

That's a simple use of small data. The opportunities and challenges grow as the size and complexity of the data sets available scale upward. We'll look at specific challenges related to Big Data in chapter 9, but it's worth asking what data is available to your marketing team today (regardless of whether it's big or small). How can you use this data to differentiate your organization? How will you speak more relevantly to your customers?

Demand Generation

We've seen tremendous advances over the last few years in the ability of organizations to target communications directly and specifically to those individuals who are most likely to purchase a product or service. For better or worse, we each leave a digital footprint behind us wherever we go. Companies are able to find out not only what we purchased, but also where and when we shopped, what else we use that might make us a good candidate for their offerings, and more. These customer profiles allow organizations to develop customized demand-generation campaigns that hit us right where and when we are most likely to purchase.

The problem is that while the technology is available to do this effectively, most organizations aren't prepared and ready to make this happen. For every online or print direct mail piece that hits us squarely between the eyes, there are a dozen that miss the mark. Often these come from big-name marketers who should know better. Personally, I get stacks of solicitations from AT&T trying to sell me their U-Verse video service, which I have not ever purchased nor expressed interest in purchasing. It's cheap for AT&T to flood mailboxes with these promotions in the hope they'll get at least a 1 or 2 percent response rate. At the same time, Comcast continues to send me almost as many e-mail and paper campaigns for its competing product—which I'm already purchasing and have been for years.

Which is worse: AT&T's unwanted barrage of solicitations to the 98 percent of us who don't care and aren't interested in its product? Or Comcast hitting up its existing customers for something those customers are already purchasing, because the company isn't targeting its mailings appropriately?

Steve Doran, vice president of marketing and membership at the National Business Officers Association (NBOA), is focused as much on engaging the organization's current members as he is on recruiting new ones. NBOA has a clearly defined audience: chief business officers of private and prep schools. Over the last four years, the organization has more than doubled the number of attendees at its annual meeting and grown its membership ranks by nearly the same percentage.

Doran says retaining new members is largely dependent on how much these individuals are exposed to all the programs and services available to them as NBOA members. He compares program introduction to joining a gym: once you've paid your dues, does anyone tell you about the exercise classes? The personal trainers? The special events that will be happening onsite? Doran focuses on making sure his members are fully exposed to all the ways they can engage with NBOA, whether they choose to use those services or not.

With a limited budget, Doran segments his prospect database. Not all prospects are created equal. By looking at a few key criteria, he can determine whether a business officer is likely to attend an event or join the association. NBOA has tiered its database into three groups: the top 25 percent, the middle 25 percent, and the bottom half.

Doran expends more money and focus on the top group. The middle group gets some attention, but the lowest group is unlikely to get much dedicated support. The process works. Doran sees that his top-tier targets really *do* engage more often.

Targeted and thoughtful demand-generation campaigns stand out from the noise. Do your campaigns fit that description? Or are you wasting time, money, and your prospects' patience with untargeted blanket campaigns?

Drivers

Back in the "good old days," brand owners drove marketing and interactions with their organization's brand. They told us what to expect from

the brand and where to go to purchase or use it. If we wanted to participate, we did so on their terms.

Not anymore. Today, the expectation is that consumers drive interactions with a brand as much as the brand's owner does. Consumers
generate content. They determine where and when they interact with a
brand. Check out the latest YouTube videos for what consumers are up to
lately, as they parody ad campaigns and brands.

Furthermore, consumers hold brands to certain standards. They
expect quick response to consumer feedback and input, as well as effective handling of problems and issues. They also expect that the brand
will flex and change to meet the needs of its target audience, the customers who know and love the brand.

One such example is offered by retailer Caribou Coffee, a Minneapolis-
based coffee chain with $262 million in revenue from nearly five hundred
company-owned locations. When Caribou Coffee decided to launch its
PERKS loyalty program in early 2014, the company knew it had to break
the mold and not offer yet another standard retail loyalty program.

The program focused on reaching a younger generation, according to
vice president of marketing Michele Vig. That's why the program Caribou Coffee launched was experiential rather than points based. The idea
was to mimic the differentiated Caribou Coffee store experience in a
loyalty experience. Customers receive rewards via e-mail or text alert in
unscheduled, unexpected ways.

Vig says much of the credit for the early adoption of the PERKS program is due to the Caribou Coffee field teams, who focused on getting
people at the store level to register. The rewards that customers received as
a result of joining the program are what kept them coming back for more.

Caribou Coffee drives engagement with customers in many different
ways. For example, customers can take a picture of themselves with their
Caribou coffee cup, telling the world how much Caribou Coffee made
their day. They share their own videos on the Caribou Coffee site, engaging at different levels as they see fit. They spend a great deal of time talking about where they are enjoying Caribou coffee—both virtually and
out and about.

Caribou Coffee likes to go where the customers are. For example, the company often shows up unexpectedly at summer sports practices with a cart that gives away "cool stuff" while serving iced lattes and carbonated drinks. The goal: become a part of the day for customers who might not otherwise be thinking about coffee. The result? Caribou Coffee's loyalty program has been a huge success. Nearly 30 percent of the customer base enrolled quickly, allowing Caribou Coffee to hit its marketing goals months ahead of schedule.

Are you going to where your customers are, rather than expecting them to drive to you? Do you engage with customers in ways that please and surprise them? Understanding key customer drivers can help you leverage your marketing efforts to move faster and more effectively in this new world.

Conversations, Content, and Communities

There's one more critical new reality to consider. And to understand it, we need to look at a book that predicted many of the changes we see in marketing today, including the development of social media. *The Cluetrain Manifesto*, first published in 1999, proclaimed "the End of Business as Usual."[4] It aimed to set businesses and marketers straight about what they needed to do differently to succeed in the new Web-centric world. The manifesto, recently called one of the "20 best marketing books of all time,"[5] has ninety-five tenets. But it's the first one that sets the stage for a key reality in today's world: Markets are conversations.

Cluetrain said that, for too long, businesses have had one-way communication with customers, treating them as recipients of information. The new reality of the Web allows us to go back to the way things were in the good old days: it lets us have conversations with real people using real voices.

Conversations are the starting point. Yes, we need to participate and engage with customers. But we also need to provide useful content (not marketing hype) to those engaging in conversations. And we need to show up in the communities where our audiences are gathering online and off.

Conversations. Content. Community. Let's look at each of these in turn.

Conversations

The era when marketers could talk *at* customers has long passed. Not only do customers want to talk *to* organizations and brands, they actually have a lot of interesting and important things to say. But it is no more enjoyable for marketers to listen to a monologue from a customer than it is for customers to listen to one from a brand. The key is to engage in *conversations*—back-and-forth discussions that veer down different paths depending on what's on the customer's mind. Do this in the same way you'd engage friends or colleagues. Find a topic of interest, ask a question, and then *listen* to the response. Take the feedback to the right parts of the organization and close the loop.

What's critical about conversation is that the customer feels heard. This doesn't require restructuring the business or changing priorities to meet customer demands. It just means the organization needs to follow a simple three-step process with those who provide feedback:

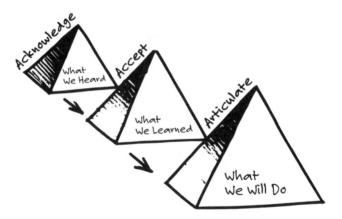

FIGURE 4-1: Acknowledge, Accept, Articulate

- **Acknowledge** that the feedback has been received.
- **Accept** that there is valuable input and information in the feedback (whether you agree with the input or not).
- **Articulate** your next steps now that you've received this input (share it with others in the organization, research the issue more deeply, make changes to a process or procedure, etc.).

A word to the wise: if your conversations with customers consistently identify the same key sticking points, it's time to consider whether you *should* change your approach. There's a pattern here, and you need to pay attention to the information you've been given.

Content

Content is a buzzword in today's marketing circles. We now see individuals with director or vice president of content as their title. But what exactly *is* content? Content is information, quite simply. It's information that customers need to make decisions to purchase your offering, to use it, or to recommend it to others. This includes not only information about your company or your product, but also details about your offerings, testimonials and user stories (good and bad), outlets where customers can purchase the product, places to get support, the "gotchas" to watch out for, and ways people are using your service to build their business.

Content also includes information that isn't directly about your organization, but is related to the way your customers live their lives or do their jobs. For example, American Express has created the OPEN Network for small business owners, which provides a wide range of useful information on issues from marketing to technology to leadership to cash flow. The one thing OPEN is *not* focused on is credit card processing. It has its own community page but also a Facebook page that, as of mid-2014, had nearly 350,000 "likes."[6]

What's important is that useful content is provided in an engaging and entertaining way. There's a whole marketing subspecialty now developing that works to identify requirements for content and looks at how content can be repurposed, when it should be updated, what format it should take, and so on.

Yet more than fifteen years after *The Cluetrain Manifesto* was first published, many organizations still struggle with how to effectively generate content. In June 2014, Forrester Research found that more than half of the B2B marketers surveyed were still "in the early stages of assembling a content strategy and executing against it."[7] Furthermore, 85 percent of those surveyed couldn't connect content to business value. As a result, according to Forrester, they "fail to create those intimate, long-term rela-tionships that will form the primary source of competitive advantage in business from now on."[8]

The key point is that the value of content, like beauty, is in the eye of the beholder. You should be providing the type of content that interests and engages customers. It should be available in multiple formats for access in various ways: as print, audio, or video; across different devices; online and off. Don't force your customers to engage with you in a prescribed way. Let them choose how and where they'll consume content. We'll look at examples of organizations that have done this well later in the book.

How do you know what content is appropriate? Again, that's where those conversations with customers—and partners—come in. Engaging with customers, watching their behavior, and understanding where you can assist them will help you create, curate, and repurpose the content that makes sense for your customers.

Communities

Communities of interest aren't new. Human beings have been creating communities around common interests since language and communi-cation skills developed, thousands of years ago. We have community centers for art, music, and sports. Much political change starts at the local level with community activists. Technology companies have had community-based user groups for years.

However, social media and online tools have made developing and joining online communities extremely simple. They also allow the reach of these communities to be more pervasive and global in nature. This has led to a proliferation of online communities—from Facebook and Twit-ter to LinkedIn and Pinterest, and many more.

It's natural that organizations want to create communities for those with a common interest in their products or services. However, commu-nities don't thrive because companies or brands decide they should exist. Organizations can certainly enable communities or empower them, but communities of like-minded individuals come together of their own accord.

How can you create the kind of cohesiveness within your customer base that creates strong bonds? How can you encourage individuals to come together to discuss your product or service? To some degree, what's said, good or bad, is not important. Often, other customers will correct inaccuracies and defend your organization without you jumping in.

In many cases, your customers have been creating their own communities for years. They've been coming together at conferences and events, or staying in contact with others with similar needs. Today, we have the technology to enable this on a much wider scale. Yet even online communities look for in-person communication. Witness Tweet-ups and Meetups, where people who meet online get together in the flesh to take conversations to the next level. Communities are a way to continue the dialog with customers by providing relevant content that can be shared and discussed among a friendly audience.

My colleague Robbie Kellman Baxter talks about how communities are changing the way we buy products and services in the new membership economy. Rather than purchasing products outright, we often become members of a site or community. "Membership is about being part of the whole," says Baxter. "A customer is outside of the business ecosystem, but a member is part of it. Just by changing the language, organizations start to generate deeper, longer-term relationships with their customers."

"Million Dollar Consultant" Alan Weiss has built a unique global community of world-class consultants. His community includes tens of thousands of people who have read his books, participated in his mentoring programs, or attended his workshops and seminars. Weiss created an online gathering place, AlansForums.com, where nearly a thousand community members post on subjects ranging from consulting practices and business development ideas to life balance, self-development, and sex, religion, & politics.

Alan's Forums provide a "virtual water cooler" for consultants, many of whom are solo practitioners. It's a place where they can connect with other consultants, share best practices, learn from others' mistakes, and interact with Weiss himself. Weiss spends time each day on the Forums, commenting on topics and responding one-on-one to "Ask Alan" questions. "My community is both an R&D machine and lab," says Weiss. "It generates ideas, ensures critical mass, and serves as an evangelistic base."

The Content Changes; the Concept Doesn't

The northeastern Pennsylvania town where I grew up was known in the nineteenth century as the birthplace of anthracite coal. But Wilkes-Barre, Pennsylvania, has another claim to fame. In November of 1972, it also became the birthplace of modern cable TV programming with the launch of the first Home Box Office (HBO) service.

HBO started out with fewer than four hundred families as subscribers. The value proposition was clear: pay a monthly fee in exchange for the ability to view full-length recent movie releases in their entirety—without editing or disruption by commercial advertisers. Today, not only are there multiple cable channels offering this service (HBO alone has thirteen channels!), but viewers can choose from satellite and streaming video channels like Netflix and Amazon Prime.

What *hasn't* changed, though, is that whether you're viewing content in a movie theater, on a television screen, or on your smartphone or tablet, there are only two main ways you can acquire content: by watching advertisements or by paying a premium to go advertising free.

Think about online games as an example. You can either download the latest hot gaming app at no charge and tolerate the ads that pop up on a regular basis, or you can pay a few dollars for the premium edition that lets you play free of pop-up advertising. The delivery mechanisms change; the basic marketing concepts behind them don't.

A New Approach to Looking at Media

Are you still thinking of media in terms of print, broadcast, and digital? Forget it. Today, marketers categorize and prioritize the media options available to them in a whole different way. The following definitions

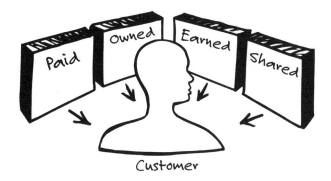

FIGURE 4-2: Today's Media

were first adopted in the digital space, but they are applicable to *all* kinds of media channels, whether or not they are online-focused.

The four categories of media channels:

Paid channels are those a brand pays to leverage, such as advertising. This includes digital display ads, pay-per-click ads, sponsorships, and offline advertising.

Owned channels, according to TopRank's *Online Marketing Blog,* are those "media, contents, and assets that the brand controls, like Websites, blogs, newsletters, and brand social media accounts. Brands are increasingly behaving like publishers with editorial staff managing content creation streams."[9]

Earned channels are built around word of mouth. According to John Lusk, writing in the *Huffington Post,* most marketers are making big investments in public relations, however delivering amazing customer experiences is a more effective means of generating awareness.[10]

Shared channels are those where consumers interact with and share content, including such sites as Facebook, Twitter, Instagram, and YouTube. According to Top Rank, "Paid and Owned Media can inspire Shared Media. Shared Media can inspire Earned Media."[11]

In September 2013, Nielsen found that 84 percent of consumers worldwide trusted word-of-mouth recommendations (earned media) from friends and family above all other sources of advertising. That's not surprising. However, Nielsen also found that traditional advertising continues to be highly trusted, with trust in TV ads increasing from 56 percent in 2007 to 62 percent in 2013.[12] According to Randall Beard, global head of advertiser solutions at Nielsen, "This emphasizes the notion that marketers maintain the ability to control the messages about their brands in a way that consumers consider credible."[13]

A well-balanced orchestra has a combination of strings, brass, woodwinds, and percussion to play orchestral pieces. But if you look carefully, you'll see that not every musician plays every piece of music on the program. Some pieces are arranged for just strings. Pieces from the Baroque period are less likely to include all the percussion and large brass sections used in later Romantic-era pieces. The experienced conductor knows he has great musicians available to him—but they don't all play at once.

Marketers need the same mind-set. We should have each of these media tools in our marketing toolbox, ready to be deployed as necessary. But we need to choose a judicious combination aligned with our goals to create the sound that will resonate with our target audiences.

Adjusting to the New Reality

Sometimes in this new reality, what was once good enough no longer works. That's what Todd Croom, former vice president of marketing and communications at NextGear Capital, found. The level of marketing presence that worked for NextGear's two predecessor companies—the used car dealer financing operations we discussed earlier—wasn't sufficient to achieve the kind of revenue growth to which the new organization aspired.

NextGear's challenge was threefold. It wanted to continue to grow its core dealer financing, or floor planning, business by attracting new customers. It wanted to grow into complementary businesses, such as financing recreational vehicle and boat sales. And it wanted existing customers to partner on a deeper level with NextGear, coming to NextGear for additional services as those customers grew their businesses. "We had to help people within our organization understand why it was so important to have a strong marketing presence," Croom said. "In some cases, this meant we had to take strong resources and leverage talents in different ways. We had people take on different roles and we coached them to take on something more tailored to what the organization needed."

Croom says it was important to educate the organization about what marketing could really do, such as building a strong analytics capability. "Before, marketing was a soft and squishy type of discipline," he said. "Now people are asking for quantitative information and analytics, what's going on with the customer, the competition. Marketing is now able to provide this for the company."

Dynamic Market Leverage Factor 2: Products

FIGURE 4-3: Dynamic Market Leverage Model—Products

Products and services are at the core of an organization's marketing strategy. These offerings are what you are bringing to market and hoping prospective customers will buy.

Product offerings are defined in many ways. Ideally, an organization finds a customer need or opportunity and creates a product or service to fill that need (even if the need is one that consumers don't yet know they have). Sometimes it is a novel product or service that first drives an organization. The company and brand come later. In too many cases, a product springs fully formed from the minds of its creators—in spite of the fact that there is no market demand for such a beast. In some cases, a first product is a hit without any testing. This leads the executive team to confuse luck with skill. They try to replicate the results, but unfortunately they very rarely draw a winning hand twice in a row.

Good strategic marketing organizations establish processes to ensure that customer input and feedback inform the product design process. This means staying close to the customer not only when determining product requirements but during design and manufacturing—to make sure that the final offering meets both usability criteria and customer needs.

We've all seen products that came to market too early—without complete functionality or full of bugs. A complete product often includes connections to complementary products or services from third parties or partners. It includes upgrade plans for existing customers and road maps to future functionality.

How important is it to get product marketing strategy right? Perhaps the best example of what happens when you *don't* follow an appropriate product strategy was the unfortunate October 2013 launch of healthcare. gov, the health insurance exchange mandated by the Affordable Care Act (Obamacare). The initial healthcare.gov Website was hampered by incomplete functionality, links to third-party insurance sites that didn't work properly, and access problems that prevented users from getting to the site at all. Furthermore, many early users started insurance applications multiple times, only to find that they were bumped out of the system or that their application never made it all the way to the insurance company of their choice. It was a mess. And it was a major embarrassment for the government, the insurance industry, and anyone connected with the project.

Part of the problem was that the team behind the Affordable Care Act implementation likely looked at the service as separate from the healthcare.gov Website. But to the consumer, the product experience started with the Website.

The Obamacare launch fiasco didn't have to happen. There was no new technology or functionality used for healthcare.gov that had not been successfully deployed by others. Companies like Amazon, Google, and Facebook come to mind when it comes to scalability and integration, and each of those handles more transactions per day than healthcare.gov would likely ever need to manage.

Imagine how different the healthcare.gov launch might have been had those in charge developed a go-to-market strategy that incorporated customer and partner feedback on the site. Consider how many problems could have been avoided with an honest assessment of launch readiness and a robust beta-testing process. Don't chalk the lack of a solid plan up to government ineptitude. Too many organizations in the private or nonprofit sectors are guilty of the same sins. The difference is that most of these episodes don't get the public scrutiny of healthcare.gov!

What processes does your organization have in place to develop the right products for your target market? How are you incorporating conversations, content, and community into your product strategy? How will you ensure that you not only obtain customer feedback but incorporate it before shipping new releases?

Customers are critical to success. Let's look at how the interactions between organizations and their key customers have changed in this new reality.

PART II

Competing for Attention

5

It All Starts with the Customer

Most organizations know who their customers are...at least on some level. But the question is, how well do they *really know* their customers?

I've been a customer of Macy's Department Stores for a long, long time. It seems every week they're sending me mailings about yet another sale. A couple of years ago, I got a notice in my bill that Macy's would soon be sending me a specialized catalog, tailored to my specific buying habits. This sounded kind of interesting. Macy's has the data to customize a catalog just for me. I've been shopping there for years. As a marketer, I was curious to see what Macy's would do with what they knew about me.

The catalog that showed up in my mailbox was disappointing. My name was printed on the front and back covers, but besides that, I couldn't figure out what about the catalog was tailored to me. It still contained baby clothes, even though my "baby" was now in college. It also contained mattresses, furniture, and menswear—even though these were not purchases I normally made at Macy's. And it contained ads for women's clothing lines I've never bought before and am not likely to buy in the future. So much for Macy's customizing its mailings for *me*. In fact, the last time I looked, even my name on the front and back cover of the catalog had disappeared. More recently, I subscribed to Target's

Cartwheel app. However, the promotions listed in the e-mails sent to me are no more personalized to my needs than Macy's paper catalogs.

The better you know your customers, the better you can target your offerings to meet their needs—ideally, before they even realize they have those needs. The more targeted you can be, the less time and money you will spend on wasteful marketing activities that don't reach the right people anyway.

To start with, a customer, as we're defining the term, is an individual, not an organization or a corporation. You may sell your services to large commercial banks, but "the bank" doesn't buy your offerings. An individual within the bank makes the purchase decision. That individual belongs to a function and has specific responsibilities. She also has personal characteristics: number of years in her current role, level of authority, scope and span of control, reporting structure, etc. Titles are not always an indication of responsibilities. In a bank, for example, everyone but the cleaning staff will likely have a title of vice president.

The more finely you can target the characteristics of the individual who makes the purchase decision, the more successful your effort will be. Who does that person interface with? Who influences him? What does he read? To which organizations does he belong ?

You'll also want to know the *context* of the typical situation in which your clients typically find themselves. Are they in growth mode? Are they cutting costs? Is this a turnaround situation? Furthermore, how will your product help your customers personally? If it's not something they will use themselves, is it for family members? A member of their team? Do they make purchases or recommendations to other teams? How will their careers be impacted—positively or negatively—by being associated with your product? We often hear about the challenges or problems a customer may face (what keeps them up at night?), but what about the potential opportunities they could conquer? How can your product change their lives and the lives of those around them?

Who Are These People and Why Are They Here?

Too many businesses fail because they develop a wonderful product or service that isn't what their target audience wants or needs. Worse yet, they develop a product that's great for everyone, which means it's targeted to no one. They market the living daylights out of it and then wonder why they still aren't successful. Often, they spend too much of their time talking *at* customers after the product is designed rather than *with* them through the entire product life cycle.

So many organizations treat their customers and prospects as if they are a necessary evil. In some ways, this makes sense. After all, customers are demanding. They want more and more of our time, ask for new features and new functionality, expect more support—and they expect all this to happen at a lower price.

Sometimes they even take our products and use them in ways we never intended. Pinterest and Facebook are filled with creative uses for everyday products—uses the original manufacturers never envisioned, let alone intended. Industrial blender manufacturer Blendtec joined in and took this creativity to an art form. There's now a near cult following for Blendtec's series of low-cost and high-fun "Will It Blend?" videos. The appeal is both visceral and visual. Will they put *that thing* in a blender? And will it really still work?

As marketers, our role starts during the product design process. It continues through the sales cycle, when we uncover leads and help convert prospects to customers. We're often called in to try to sell additional products and services to existing customers. But customers want attention beyond that—they want attention *all the time.* Is that our job? Where does marketing stop and customer support begin? Wouldn't life be easier without all these people demanding things from us? Well, not exactly.

The Good, the Bad, and the WIIFM

Make no mistake about it: customers don't care about you. They don't care about how great you are, the extensive talent and experience in your organization, or how successful you've been in the past. Unless, that is, that information ties to helping *them,* the customers.

If your success can make *me* more successful, then, as a customer, I care. If your experience can help me avoid pitfalls, that's important. But the bottom line is that customers want to know, "What's in it for me?" This is a phenomenon we affectionately call the WIIFM.

Too often, I see organizations focus on *their* strengths or the features in their product or service offerings, without clearly articulating why these things are important for their customers. What's the benefit to the customer of the great functionality you're building into your product? This may vary by industry, by product type, and by customer, but customers are usually looking for a few simple things:

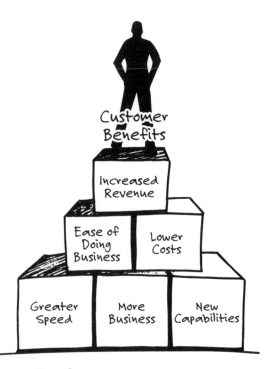

FIGURE 5-1: Customer Benefits

- Will the product/service bring more revenue?
- Will it make my life easier?
- Will it cut costs?
- Will it let me move faster?
- Will it help me attract more customers? Will it let me introduce new capabilities I didn't have before?

Just about every other benefit can be derived from at least one of these six. For example, introducing a mobile app may not bring incremental revenue, but it's likely to cut costs, improve quality, and introduce new capabilities.

Ask whether there's a good match between what your organization is prepared to offer and what your customer needs. The way to know this is to really get to know your customer, up close and personal.

Chief Customer Officers: The Buck Stops Here

There's a new kid in the C-suite town: the chief customer officer. For decades, organizations have had individuals on the executive team with accountability for shareholders, operations efficiencies, R&D, and revenue—but not for customers. The chief customer officer (CCO) is responsible for helping the organization be accountable to customers for company decisions—from strategy to product design to service design to delivery.

Curtis Bingham, founder and president of the Chief Customer Officer Council, is at the forefront of the movement to create and empower chief customer officers. Ten years ago, when Bingham and I first discussed his idea for a CCO Council, there were a mere thirty people in the world who had the CCO title. By 2014, there were more than four hundred officially named CCOs globally—and hundreds more doing similar work without the official title. The first CCOs were found mainly in larger, enterprise companies. Today, the title appears in a broad range of organizations, including small- to medium-sized companies (less than $1 billion in annual revenue) and nonprofit organizations.

One of the first people to embody the CCO concept was Marissa Peterson at Sun Microsystems. Peterson's official title was executive vice president of worldwide operations, but over time she also took on the role of chief customer advocate in order to address systemic customer problems at Sun. Reporting directly to the CEO, Peterson architected and implemented programs to drive "voice of the customer" requirements into Sun's business processes. She was the senior executive responsible for resolving red alert issues with customers. The buck stopped with Peterson. Sun executives knew it and so did their customers.

Today the CCO and the CMO are often peers. Bingham sees the CCO's role as critical once demand-generation activities have yielded a sales contract. Because the CCO's focus is often on post-sales customer interactions, he'll often have valuable insights for marketing and should be seen as a strong ally. This is someone who can bring the voice of the customer to those areas of the organization that need to hear it, according to Bingham. The CCO can provide valuable feedback to the marketing team in terms of what is and is not resonating with customers. And he can introduce a longer-term view into the lifetime interactions an organization has with its customers.

A laser focus on customers is one way organizations stand out above the noise. Does your organization have a CCO? If not, what can you, as a marketing leader, do to help create the single-minded focus on customers that will help your organization market above the noise?

Customer Complaints Are Not to Be Ignored

It's logical to think that customer complaints should be avoided at all costs. After all, who wants to have dissatisfied customers airing their dissatisfaction to the world? But the one thing that's less desirable than complaining customers is unhappy customers who *don't* complain. That's because the people who don't complain are the folks who get frustrated and literally take their ball (and their business) and go home. You don't hear from them; they just disappear. You may not have even known they were upset with you before they vanished.

A customer with a complaint is one who cares enough about you and your organization to stay engaged with you through thick and thin. He wants to make sure you know there's a problem. He wants to be heard, and he wants you to make things better, because he has a relationship with you that he'd like to preserve if possible.

Think about the times you've been asked by a merchant about your experience: Did you find everything you were looking for? Were the accommodations to your satisfaction? Most of the time you likely said, yes, everything's fine—whether or not that was true. If you were dissatisfied, you might have said things were fine for two reasons: (1) you were not actively engaged with that merchant or (2) you didn't think things would change anyway, so why bother wasting the time and energy? A customer who voices her dissatisfaction is both engaged with you and of the mind that her input will be heard and will make some kind of difference in the organization.

I recently stayed at a brand-new Marriott Hotel in the Los Angeles area. The facilities were great but the service was not. Because I often stay at properties owned by the Marriott chain, I have a vested interest in telling them when something's not right. So I called the manager aside and politely explained why it was unacceptable that my room was not cleaned before 5 p.m. each day—especially after I had raised this issue on day one with the desk clerk.

The manager apologized, agreed that the new staff likely needed additional training, and refunded a good portion of my charges. I left feeling that my voice had been heard and there was a reasonable chance that changes would be made because of my complaint.

Many companies have adopted the Net Promoter Score (NPS), developed by Fred Reichheld, to measure customer engagement and satisfaction. Net Promoter Scores look at how much each customer is promoting your brand or organization. One strategy companies use to maximize their score is to eliminate interactions with customers who aren't giving them high scores. The problem is that those customers who care enough to rate you lower may be sending an important message, one you need to hear loud and clear. Paying more attention to those who lavish praise on you is good for the ego, but it also means putting on blinders and limiting your peripheral vision. You're likely to miss what's happening off to the side that may impact you.

Organizations that rise above the noise solicit customer input, good and bad, and they act on it to improve their performance and drive their marketing.

What *You* Want Isn't Always Relevant

When I first came to Sun Microsystems in the late 1980s, our business was fairly simple. We made the technical workstations that powered engineering and scientific computation, as well as computer-aided design. That made it easy to design and build products: our customers were people just like our engineers.

Even when Sun workstations became the rage on Wall Street, we were safe. Wall Street firms had started hiring rocket scientists to figure out the computing algorithms that made trading systems work. They were still engineers, but they dressed better.

It was when we moved into business and commercial markets that we had to stop and reconsider. Not only were we selling to people with a different set of goals and objectives, we were selling to users who had a different experience base. They wanted a more intuitive user interface and less involvement with the technology. We had to ask customers what they wanted, because they were no longer us.

Too often, marketers think they know who their customers are and what they want. But it turns out they usually know only part of the story. The best way to find out what your customers want? Ask. Customers love to tell you what's on their mind, how they run their businesses, what their business processes are, etc. All you have to do is ask them...and listen to their responses.

The assumptions we make about why our customers buy from us aren't always correct. As a consultant, I'm often brought in to conduct research with customers or partners on behalf of a client. Customers will tell me things they wouldn't say to the organization directly. As a third party, I am asking for and receiving information without judgment. I'm not defensive when they tell me my client screwed up, and I'm not attempting to sell or cajole them in any way.

One of my favorite questions when conducting this type of interview is why customers purchase from a client. The insights I gain are profound. Sometimes what I learn matches nicely with what the customer thinks is important, but other times there are other agendas, issues, or concerns raised. We learn these things mainly because we ask. A customer responds and we ask more deeply to learn even more. Ask your customers to talk honestly with you. You'll be surprised what you find out.

Go to Market Means Go to Customers

Boots is the U.K.'s leading pharmacy-led health and beauty retailer with just under 2,500 stores across the U.K. Customer strategy is at the heart of what Boots does, says retail and brands strategy director Simon Potts. "We always start with what is it about the brand and our communications that's right," he says. "We're also fundamentally trying to understand the big picture with consumers—trends, how consumers are behaving, what they're liking and not liking—so that everything we do adds meaningful value toward those things."

Boots, a member of Alliance Boots, the international pharmacy-led health and beauty group, was an early adopter of loyalty card programs, introducing its Boots Advantage Card program in 1997. Today, the company has nearly eighteen million loyalty members that it connects with on a regular basis. Feedback from these customers changes the way the company implements and executes promotions in its stores, and it affects product development for the company's own brands.

How does this impact the company's marketing strategies? According to Potts, Boots seeks to identify insights for the target audience around a particular theme, such as Christmas or summer vacation. Only once that insight has been determined does the company craft the content for marketing campaigns—including what is offered to customers, the price range, and the promotions.

"These insights directly impact not just what we advertise in media, but what we actually offer customers in the first place, how we lay out our stores, and what promotions we have," Potts says. He notes the business believes in a customer-led organization. Note that Potts doesn't say marketing-led, but *customer*-led.

Its customer focus means that Boots won't support a major launch of a vendor's products if the company doesn't see that product as being genuinely good for Boots customers. Because Boots, as a retailer, sells both its own products and other major brands, the company believes there are many different ways it can delight and engage with consumers. "We genuinely believe in partnership. If the supplier is one that is seeking to add value in the category in which they're operating—if they want to add value to customers—then we want to share insights both ways in order to make that happen," Potts says.

Boots engages customers in two ways. First, the company holds regular customer panels at each store, inviting customers in to talk about what's working and what's not. Second, it chooses an individual store to use as a test lab. Teams will develop new initiatives, perhaps twenty a day, and stage them in an actual store to see the reactions from customers. Rather than go through a long development cycle, Potts says, they'll quickly redesign a store to get instant responses to the new layout, as well as to the new products introduced that day.

The key focus, Potts notes, is that Boots puts customer strategy at the heart of what they do. "Some take a transactional approach to customer strategy, which says, how do we make the most money out of customers?" says Potts. "We really seek to do the right thing for our customers."

The Cult of the Newly Converted

A funny thing happens when you delight customers. They get so excited they have to talk about it again and again. In today's environment, audiences are bigger and more widely dispersed. Plus, it's easy to let everyone know what's on your mind.

A new customer engagement is almost like the start of a romantic relationship. There's excitement and anticipation and the sense that anything is possible. Actually, this *is* a new relationship—but with an organization or a brand rather than with another human being. Just as on the personal side, though, mismatches between early expectations and reality can doom a new relationship before it even gets off the ground. It's important to leverage this honeymoon period. Make it easy and enjoyable for customers to talk about you, refer you, and take the next steps to sustain and deepen the relationship.

Your marketing should reinforce the wisdom of the customer's choice. A good portion of automotive advertising is targeted at those who have recently purchased a vehicle. Why? To reinforce the feeling that they've made the right purchase decision. This is critical because when the new car smell starts to wear off, buyer's remorse sets in. And that's about the time someone asks the new car owner what she thinks of her BMW or Prius or KIA or Ford Explorer. Would she recommend it? Car manufacturers know that they need to get people thinking about the next car as soon as they've purchased a vehicle.

What about your business? How are you working to make customers feel good that they've teamed up with your organization? Internet retailer Zappos takes customer satisfaction to another level by guaranteeing they'll be satisfied with their online shoe purchase. And, if they're not—if a pair of shoes doesn't fit right or if the customer just doesn't like them once she's seen them up close and personal—no problem. She can return them for a refund. Return shipping is free, too.

Zappos has been so successful at building a powerful, positive customer experience that Amazon gave the company one of the highest possible compliments—it bought Zappos but left the shoe retailer to operate as it always had. Amazon knew the Zappos business model was firing on all cylinders.

Today Zappos has created a side business inviting other businesses and organizations to visit its Las Vegas headquarters for a tour of the Zappos customer service model. Zappos Insights is a group that's chartered with sharing the Zappos culture and experience with other organizations. Why? According to the Zappos Website, "We believe any workplace can benefit from identifying and/or strengthening their own culture and core values."[1]

Saboteurs Will Kill You Every Time

We know about the power of customer evangelists, who feel they "own" your brand and proselytize for you to others. But what about the folks who are not as enthralled?

Some of the people who don't idolize your brand will remain customers because they have no choice. Many people can't choose their electric utility or cable provider, for example. For a long time, the only real choice of operating system for personal computers was the one made by Microsoft. Many of us put up with a less-than-ideal user experience because we felt we had no feasible alternative.

What's interesting is that the market evolves to give us alternatives. There may still be only one cable provider in your area, but today you can purchase similar services from Direct TV via satellite, or you can stream video directly from Netflix, Amazon, or other similar services. Over the past decade, many people moved from PCs to Macs. Now, with tablets and smartphones proliferating, they're abandoning personal computers entirely.

These alternatives evolve because there are unmet needs in the market. The lesson here is twofold. First, be aware of what's making your customers unhappy, before someone else jumps in with a better option. Second, look at the environment and find areas where other suppliers are leaving a wake of bad feelings. They're creating a great potential opportunity for you.

Dynamic Market Leverage Factor 3: Customers

FIGURE 5-2: Dynamic Market Leverage Factor—Customers

It sounds simple: without customers, we don't have a sustainable business. Yet many organizations take their customers for granted or treat them like a necessary evil.

Not all customers are created equal. Some are much more profitable to have than others. Some should be jettisoned as soon as possible. Others can possibly be nurtured into more attractive long-term targets. It's important to have a process in place to define the characteristics of your ideal customers. You should know who they are, what makes them more attractive, and why they come to you rather than your competitors.

What is a customer worth to you over the lifetime of your relationship with him? What does it cost you to acquire each customer? What is the damage to your organization if they leave before you've had the opportunity to build a lasting relationship? What are the key drivers of loyalty among your critical customers? It's one thing to listen to customer input, it's another to act on it in a meaningful way. Successful organizations have mechanisms in place to absorb customer input and make it actionable throughout the organization.

Stop and look at the customers who admire you. How well are you identifying, cultivating, leveraging, and rewarding those individuals who become advocates for you and your brand? Note that not all rewards are monetary in nature. Customer advocates want to feel acknowledged and appreciated.

Put your money where your mouth is. Measure and promote activities that lead employees to engage with your customers in positive ways. Customers may want to be seen as innovators and thought leaders—among their peers and in their communities. Perhaps they want early access to new products or technology you have in development. Maybe they just want the cachet of being closely associated with a brand they admire and respect. Look at how thousands of people converge on Apple stores the first day a new product is available. They're not getting anything the rest of us won't get a few days later—except the right to say they were there first.

To drive this kind of customer engagement, it's important that your own customer-facing personnel are encouraged to meet customer needs autonomously and effectively. They should not hesitate to take the extra step to resolve a customer issue, or, more importantly, to prevent one from occurring. Employees know when the organization really is passionate about serving customers and when the talk is just lip service.

6

Reputation Is the New Black:
Branding Above the Noise

What kind of relationships do consumers have with brands? In 2009, PepsiCo's Americas Beverages division redesigned the carton of its popular Tropicana Pure Premium orange juice. The change was to the packaging only: the product itself remained *exactly* the same. The familiar illustration of an orange with a straw was replaced by a large glass of orange juice, as part of an overall rebranding of the product.

The backlash was quick and dramatic. Sales plummeted nearly 20 percent. Consumer reaction was so negative that the company went back to the old look in only a matter of weeks. Neil Campbell, president of Tropicana Beverages North America, said, "We underestimated the deep emotional bond" consumers have with the original packaging. The cost of scrapping the new look was estimated to be in the millions of dollars.[1]

Think that was bad? Consider this. In October 2010, the Gap introduced a more modern logo. This ill-fated effort lasted a mere *two days* before the online backlash forced the company to go back to the familiar white GAP letters on a navy blue background. At least the Gap made the decision to return to the original logo quickly, before there had been time to make any new marketing materials.[2]

For businesses, this is scary. Not only do we have to move quickly to bring products to market and promote them, but we have to be prepared to react even faster to customer feedback, because our customers *expect* us to listen and respond. And it can all blow up in our faces.

Branding today requires looking beyond the traditional mind-set and branding techniques that have driven marketers for generations. Branding is now about holding conversations with customers and prospects. It's about moving quickly not just to establish a brand identity but to react when there's an incident that could cause negative reactions. It means building a brand reputation both online and off. It means asking customers what they think your brand should be. And it means thinking globally. At all times.

Let's look at each of these elements in this chapter.

Why Word of Mouth Matters More Today

Branding takes on a whole new significance in a world where everyone and everything has a reputation. The new branding isn't just about logos or typefaces or tag lines. It includes reputation management, both online and off. This has significant implications for marketers in a world where it's amazingly easy for everyone to become critics—even when the information they relay is inaccurate or out of date.

Word of mouth has always been part of the sales and marketing process. Today, mass media channels are no longer the main vehicles that deliver brand messages. Buyers trust their peers and communities much more than they trust us, the marketers. Now that the technology is available to share thoughts and views widely and instantly, it's expected that everyone and his brother will participate.

Now that brands can touch an exponential number of people, word of mouth takes on a greater significance. Marketers are expected to listen carefully to what customers tell them. Consumers expect brands to respond quickly and effectively, even instantly; their reactions are amplified through the social channels and communities that sprout up on an ongoing basis.

Exposing the Good, the Bad, and the Ugly

Coldwell Banker Bain Seal, located in Seattle, Washington, is the second-largest independent franchisee of the global Coldwell Banker real estate chain. CMO Suzanne Zinn Mueller is responsible for both B2B and B2C marketing. Her B2B audience is the agents affiliated with the firm, who are independent contractors. The B2C audience is the individuals who buy and sell homes in the Pacific Northwest. Marketing to agents is fairly utilitarian: it's important to make sure "the plumbing" works—and it has to work well, according to Mueller.

Marketing to consumers, however, requires creativity. Mueller realized that even though prospective buyers might not contact the firm until three months before they are seriously interested in buying a home, there are actually multiple phases in the seven- to ten-year cycle between imagining owning a home and making an offer. She understood that building relationships with home buyers and sellers long before they were ready to complete a real estate transaction was key to differentiating Coldwell Banker Bain Seal from other brokerages in the area. The firm's new Website focuses on the story of a new home, from dream to reality, and shepherds people through the various stages of envisioning a new home—not just serving up current listings, as other brokerage sites do.

In 2013, Mueller instituted a first-in-the-nation process for a real estate brokerage: surveying *everyone* who had completed a transaction with Coldwell Banker Bain Seal and publishing *all* of the responses— good, bad, and ugly—on the firm's Website, as well as on the company Facebook page. Coldwell Banker Bain Seal also asked clients to post their reviews on Yelp, Google Plus, and other online review sites.

The survey program, managed by a third-party firm, was piloted with a small group of agents to see how well the process would be received. According to Mueller, Coldwell Banker Bain Seal was stunned by how well the survey worked—so much so that she was deluged by agents asking to have *their* transactions rated, too.

Bad reviews are positive in three ways, according to Mueller. First, they provide an opportunity to reengage with a client. Second, they provide credibility (who has confidence in the veracity of reviews that are all excellent?). Third, they allow agents to showcase their ability to provide service, skills, and professionalism in their response to customers. The key was to train agents in how to respond to less-than-glowing reviews. Coldwell Banker Bain Seal advises agents to take the conversation offline and to understand what the client was really communicating about her real estate experience.

Mueller's goal: to use online word of mouth to build a solid corporate reputation...one transaction at a time.

Response Time: Is Yesterday Soon Enough?

One of the peculiarities of today's marketing environment is that time frames have been compressed tremendously. Technology allows us to receive communications and to tap into the wider world on a rapid basis. With mobile devices, we are never really away from multiple sources of information.

Consumers also have a greatly reduced attention span. In the golden age of TV advertising, most commercials were sixty seconds. Today, that seems like an eternity. Outside of special occasions (like the Super Bowl), it's unusual to see a sixty-second spot. Try timing the ads next time you're watching TV. They're likely to be fifteen or thirty seconds—that's all. A great percentage of potential viewers never watch the ads at all, since they set their DVRs to fast-forward through commercial breaks.

Twitter set a faster pace when it limited posts to 140 characters or fewer. Then came Vine, which limits videos to no more than six seconds. That makes some two- or three-minute YouTube videos feel long. And forget about those that are longer. It's unlikely they'll find an audience who will watch them from beginning to end.

Because marketers are reaching out to consumers on a rapid, 24–7 basis, consumers expect to be able to get the same kind of rapid response to their questions and concerns. If they have an issue with something they read or hear, they want to comment and know someone's listening to them. If they have a bad customer experience, consumers want to tweet about it to the responsible organization and know someone on the other end is paying attention—right now. As marketers, we are expected to be listening and responding all the time. If not, the noise level rises dramatically—and it's almost impossible to be heard.

How you respond to real-time branding challenges—positive or negative—can have a major impact on whether your organization rises above the noise or gets lost in nasty interference.

Quick Reflexes Build Reputation

It was a moment that all event producers dread. There you are, at the most watched television event of the year, when the power in the stadium suddenly and mysteriously disappears. That's what happened during the 2013 Super Bowl in New Orleans between the San Francisco 49ers and the Baltimore Ravens. While the local audience sat in the dark and television viewers pondered what went wrong, Oreo cookies jumped on the situation with a flash of brilliance. The brand's timely tweet: *Power out? No problem. You can still dunk in the dark.*

What's more impressive is that Oreo was not even a Super Bowl advertiser. But the company had a social media team watching the game and looking for opportunities to jump in with timely and relevant content. That's a touchdown with extra point conversion for a cookie brand.[3]

Dealing with Reputation Backlash

Contrast Oreo's attention to customer mood with the misadventures of Susan G. Komen, previously known as the Susan G. Komen Breast Cancer Foundation. This charity hit major turbulence in 2011 when it discontinued financial grants for breast health screening to Planned Parenthood because Planned Parenthood's services included abortions.

The backlash was swift and harsh. Thousands of women boycotted Komen's well-known Race for the Cure fund-raising events for breast cancer research. Social media were abuzz with the story for months. Komen founder Nancy Brinker resigned, but rescinding the decision didn't help restore Komen's reputation.[4] According to Harris Interactive, in 2012, Komen suffered a 21 percent drop in brand equity from the previous year—dropping fifty-four spots to fifty-sixth place out of seventy-nine nonprofits in its annual survey of nonprofit reputation.[5]

Planned Parenthood fared much better. Not only did the organization eventually regain the original $680,000 in funding Komen had cut, but across the country Planned Parenthood organizations received more than $3 million in *additional* donations as a result of the publicity—all of which it directed to a new breast health initiative.[6]

Other breast cancer–related charities benefited, too. Two years later, many women have changed their allegiance from Komen's Race for the Cure to events like Avon's Breast Cancer Walk.

Conversations Versus Control

To get above the noise, marketers need to understand what they can and can't do when it comes to driving brands. Many organizations relied in the past on a "command-and-control" approach to marketing. *We* will tell *you* what you need to know about our brand. We'll control how our brands are used, as well as where and when they appear. No doubt about it—we're in charge.

That may work well for the military, but it doesn't work in today's business environment. As marketers, we can't control what's said about our brands, but we *can* listen and observe what's happening.

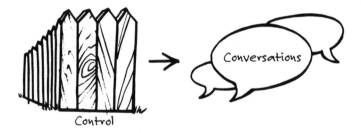

FIGURE 6-1: Control Versus Conversations

Are you participating in the conversations happening in your markets? Are you responding to issues as they arise? Are you raising questions and creating the opportunity for stimulating discussion?

There's one caveat to remember: these conversations may not be representative of the customer population as a whole. That's why, now more than ever, you need to continue to reach out and understand what customers like and don't like about your brand. Elicit opinions from those on the sidelines, as well as listening to those who are monopolizing the conversation.

It takes a long time to build a brand reputation...and a short time to destroy it. Let's look at what happened to JCPenney in just a few short months.

JCPenney: How *Not* to Update Your Brand

In mid-2011, JCPenney, a 109-year-old retailer, decided it was time to change its business strategy dramatically. The company hired Ron Johnson, who architected the retail strategy for one of today's most successful retailers, Apple. He was given a mandate to change Penney's, and change it he did—from top to bottom.

Johnson updated the store name to JCP and introduced a new white and red cubed logo. He changed the layout of Penney stores by creating a collection of separate boutiques. He also changed the Penney product mix. According to *Fortune* magazine, the new JCP "featured a much higher percentage of branded merchandise—modern, higher-end, youth-oriented—compared with house brands."[7]

This was a surprise to Penney's customer base. The middle-class moms who made up JCPenney's most loyal shoppers were shocked to find that many of their more affordable favorite brands quickly disappeared. This included St. John's Bay, a private-label brand that had generated $1 billion in annual revenue for the retailer.[8]

The biggest change, however, was in the way Penney did business. Gone were the ongoing sales, promotions, and clearances that Penney's customers expected. In their place were three prices for each item: an original low price, a month-long value price, and a twice-a-month "best" price for items the store really wanted to move.[9]

According to Kusum Ailawadi, professor of marketing at Dartmouth's Tuck School of Business, the new strategy may have implied low cost, but customers found it more expensive. Penney took away the deals that had attracted customers to the store and made them feel like smart shoppers. And, because the everyday prices weren't reduced enough, shoppers most likely paid a higher net price than before.[10]

"The appeal of the redesigned JCPenney store is simply not strong enough to offset this," said Ailawadi. "There is too much competition right around the corner. This is very different from Apple, which is highly differentiated and controls distribution and retail price points so that one cannot go to the store next door and find the same product at a lower price."[11]

Ailawadi was right. Sixteen months and more than $1 billion in losses later, Johnson was out. JCP was gone. JCPenney was back, and so were many of the promotions. The chain continued to struggle, however, both in terms of revenues and profits. In early 2014, pricing issues were front and center again. An employee was fired after publicly proclaiming that Penney had bumped up prices of some items so it could then appear to discount them.[12]

It's not clear whether JCPenney will survive. The company has lost market share, billions of dollars, and the goodwill of its customers. In mid-2014, when the stock market was hitting all-time highs, JCPenney stock was at a bargain basement price not seen since the early 1980s.

There are many lessons to be learned here. Let's focus on the ones related to branding. First, brands are not built in a vacuum. They require a strong brand promise that resonates with an organization's target market.

Second, the tactics that made specific organizations successful (in this case, Apple) can't be replicated as-is across other organizations. Marketers who get above the noise understand they need to *adapt* techniques to their specific situation, not *adopt* them wholesale.

Finally, before you start changing your brand, be sure you know the values your new brand will project. Understand how it will play with your existing customer base. JCPenney didn't like its old brand. But when the company started cleaning house, it dumped not just old store layouts, but customer trust, too.

According to Robin Lewis, CEO of retail industry newsletter *The Robin Report*, when the deal experience disappeared, betrayed shoppers disappeared, too. "They threw their hands up, shut their wallets and walked out the front door," Lewis said.[13]

Leveraging Brand Experiences Worldwide

When you do get a brand right, it's important that that branding experience be consistent wherever the brand is sold, worldwide. Steve Johnson will tell you he has "the best job on the planet." As the global brand director for Wrigley's Skittles candy, he's responsible for ensuring that brand assets are used consistently and effectively in all the countries where Skittles are sold. And Skittles is a product that works everywhere. That includes China (Skittles' second-largest market) and Russia, as well as Europe and Latin America.

Johnson says a key focus of his job is driving simplification. He spends a great deal of time questioning why marketing managers are doing what they do. Is there an easier way to do that? Are there creative assets that can be leveraged? Can designs for display vehicles be created on a regional level, allowing local marketers to put in elements that are most relevant for their specific market?

Often, local marketers can overcomplicate what they're doing, which drives cost and complexity. It can also result in marketing campaigns that waste valuable time and money. Johnson says his Canadian team did a complicated promotion that required customers to watch a three-minute video and then forward the video to others. The U.K. team, on the other hand, created a much simpler promotion offering Facebook users the opportunity to win the last Skittle produced in 2012.

Johnson says part of his focus is to provide the Skittles marketing team with examples of global communications, both good and bad. He'll show the business results, hold up what went right and wrong, and discuss what can be learned from the experience. His senior management is okay with failure, as long as the manager or team fails fast and learns from the process.

One issue Johnson sees is that marketers get bored with things very easily. Consumers may not have even seen a product or promotion, but the marketers who have done the work are so familiar with the campaign that they're tired of it. Sometimes the product may not even be on the shelf yet. Many campaigns run effectively for three to four years before being replaced. Marketers have to understand that their fatigue with a marketing campaign doesn't necessarily translate to consumers.

Johnson notes that the Internet is a great tool for testing. Rather than spending a year developing a campaign in a vacuum, he can put it on the Web and test it within days. Did people participate? Did they like it? Did they tweet about it?

What Johnson's team is doing must be working. Skittles brand sales have more than doubled in the last five years, and the company's goal is to nearly double those figures again by 2017. In fact, Wrigley can't make the product fast enough. A new factory opened in 2014 in Europe, with additional factories coming online in the United States and China in 2015.

Johnson has no qualms about the value of his product: "We're clear this is a candy, not a health food. There's no pretense about that." He has one request for you: "Could you buy just one package of Skittles a month . . . or at least maybe one package a year?"

Repairing Reputation the Old-Fashioned Way

Not all reputation building happens online. Tony Cancelosi, president and CEO of the Columbia Lighthouse for the Blind, located in the Washington, D.C., area, had his work cut out for him when he joined the organization in 2005. Columbia Lighthouse is a 114-year-old institution with a mission to help those who have lost their sight. At one point, the organization sold light bulbs door-to-door to raise money to offer services.

When Cancelosi arrived, he needed to reevaluate many aspects of the organization. Columbia had strong name recognition, longevity, and a reputation for serving people. In fact, more than 80 percent of the organization's staff are vision impaired.

Yet Columbia Lighthouse needed to evolve to fit the times. Its mission expanded to include the visually impaired as well as those who are totally blind. And rather than selling products to raise money, the organization now focuses on helping the blind and visually impaired achieve independence. Many of the agencies that Columbia worked with had an outdated view of the organization. It was time to re-brand and re-market the organization to get the message out.

Because his budget was limited, Cancelosi decide to work on perceived deficiencies. He focused on improving the quality of his "product offering" and the services available. He also added incremental capacity to serve additional constituents. Once he'd done this, Cancelosi was able to reach out to the agencies that had seen Columbia in the old way and rebuild the organization's reputation.

Today, Columbia touches four to five thousand people annually, reaching them not just once but two or three times a year. The organization has a solid reputation. In 2013, the organization won a quality award for performance from the state of Maryland for its outstanding service to the local community.

What Does the Ideal Bank Look Like?

If you're not sure that the key components of your brand promise resonate with customers, there's one sure way to find out. Ask them.

SunTrust is a financial institution that dates to 1811. In the 1980s, Trust Company of Georgia and SunBank of Florida merged to form SunTrust Bank, but they continued to operate under separate names. By the mid-1990s, the decision was made to adopt the SunTrust name across all operating units. In the early 2000s, the bank realized its desire to be a full-service bank was hindered by the image of SunTrust as a stodgy, conservative institution focused on wealthier clientele.

As senior vice president for brand management and marketing services, Mike Siegel drove a strategic review of the SunTrust brand. To get above the noise, SunTrust asked if it could be the ideal bank that people wanted—a bank that did the right thing for its customers—what would that look like? SunTrust conducted surveys across all industries and lines of services. The insights, according to Siegel, were profound. The bank learned that there were five key things people wanted from a financial institution that did the right thing.

1. They wanted to be acknowledged without judgment.
2. They wanted to be shown respect, regardless of their net worth.
3. They wanted to see mutuality of effort: "Show me you will put the same effort into managing my hard-earned cash that I did in earning it."
4. They wanted to gain knowledge, so they could make better financial decisions.

5. They wanted to be reassured about the safety and security of their ideals: "Help me maintain the security of my dreams, whether I am saving for a new home, college, retirement, or something else."

Once SunTrust knew this, it put together a new brand promise, one that looked beyond money. The marketing team then needed to translate this brand promise to the company's various clienteles. What did the promise mean for each type of customer? The bank also looked for ways it might be violating these principles. Where was it making mistakes? How could these situations be avoided?

The result was a rapid increase in consumer awareness and understanding of the SunTrust value proposition. Another acquisition led to the decision to invest in new signage and address the visual brand identity. SunTrust preserved the existing core wordmark but added a sunburst icon, which brought humanity, warmth, personality, and light to the brand. The five key tenets of the brand promise were taken forward as well. "It was such a clear beacon—this was our North Star. Everybody got it," said Siegel.

Dynamic Market Leverage Factor 4: Brand

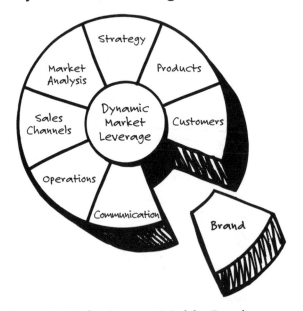

FIGURE 6-2: Dynamic Market Leverage Model—Brand

The difference between a $2 cup of coffee and a $4.50 vente soy latte at Starbucks is not the coffee or other ingredients. It's the brand.

Building and protecting your brand and reputation are critical to your organization's marketing success. This process starts with a clear understanding of your brand identity, value proposition, and positioning. Test brand identity with your employees first. If the people who know you most intimately can't easily articulate who you are and what you stand for, you've got a major problem.

Your customers, your prospects, and the key influencers in your industry or market should all be keenly aware of your organization's value proposition. It's important that the actions your company takes reinforce the position you've chosen.

Very few people were likely surprised by Whole Foods' decision to label and eventually eliminate genetically modified organisms (GMOs) from its shelves by 2018. That policy is congruent with the Whole Foods brand, and the explicit announcement reinforced what consumers expect from Whole Foods.

If, on the other hand, Whole Foods had decided to start selling artificially sweetened soft drinks, the customer outrage would have been particularly loud. This is in spite of the fact that a good proportion of Whole Foods customers likely indulge in artificially sweetened drinks on a regular basis (which they currently have to buy at another grocery store). But "artificial" is clearly not part of the Whole Foods brand. The messages that come from your organization should be consistent with your brand... and with each other.

In early 2014, CVS announced it was going to stop selling tobacco products, forgoing nearly $2 billion in annual revenue. Why? Because the chain didn't see tobacco sales as matching the health and wellness brand it is nurturing. (And it turns out tobacco sales were less than 2 percent of CVS's total revenue, so it was not a hard decision to make.)[14]

Brands are living entities. They evolve and grow over time. It's important to maintain an ongoing focus on developing and building the brand, based on an understanding of your customers' needs and perceptions. It's important that your organization puts processes in place to measure brand awareness and reputation on a regular basis. Don't wait to manage your brand until there's a crisis. You want to make small course correc-tions before things get out of hand.

Finally, it's important to have a way to close the loop in terms of bringing brand feedback into your organization. Once you've learned something relevant, be sure the input is communicated to those groups who may be impacted by the information. Asking for input and then not using it is wasteful and dangerous. Don't squander your brand equity by sitting on input, good or bad, that can help drive your organization forward.

7

Demand Generation: Getting the Message Heard

If a marketing campaign lands in a forest and there's no one there to hear it...does it make a sound? Today's organizations arm their sales and marketing teams with customer data, engage their frontline employees, and still launch marketing campaigns that fall flat. With all the resources and technology available, why does this happen? Probably because too many organizations are focused on getting their messages in front of prospective customers. What they are often *not* doing sufficiently is developing tactics that cut through the noise so those prospects are willing and able to listen to those messages.

Demand generation today is about finding the right vehicles and tactics to reach customers. That means creating and curating content that interests them, offering incentives that encourage trial, creating integrated multi-touch marketing campaigns, and measuring the results to learn what steps to take next.

We'll look at each of these areas in this chapter.

Generating Demand Through Content Marketing

You don't have to have a large marketing budget to generate demand through content marketing. Let's look at the examples of Zillow and LawBiz Management.

With data on more than 110 million U.S. homes, Zillow.com is today the leading home and real estate marketplace on the Web and mobile. But the company faced a very different challenge when it launched in early 2006. There was no online real estate category. Furthermore, six months after launching the company, the real estate market crashed, beginning the largest housing recession in a lifetime.

Rather than just get above the noise, Zillow had to actually *create* enough sound to interest consumers, real estate agents, government agencies, and everyone else associated with the real estate market. The company had to get its audiences to pay attention to the new kid on the block.

CMO Amy Bohutinsky didn't have the budget for paid media. A former journalist who had moved into public relations, she decided to focus on earned channels. Given the new economic reality, Zillow told people the truth about what was happening in the real estate market. Things were bad and they might not get better for several years. At that time, no one else was presenting real estate data in such an unbiased way.

Zillow started to build housing reports, beginning with quarterly reports for a handful of cities. Over time the number of cities grew, as did the types of data in the reports. The company got its research into the hands of anyone who needed to use or disseminate housing data. Soon academics, economists, and government housing groups, in addition to journalists, were citing Zillow data.

Zillow knew the data had to be sound. It built a strong data science team, including PhD-level statisticians who knew how to work with data. The company's chief economist works hand in hand with the Zillow PR team. He's testified before Congress and is a regular fixture on news shows that talk about the housing market.

Bohutinsky relied on her PR background to create what became practically an in-house newsroom. Zillow had a staff of journalists turning out stories for media outlets hungry for content. Once it had a solid base, the team reached out to other media outlets, offering syndicated content at no charge. Such publications as the *Huffington Post, Yahoo Finance,* ABC News, *Business Insider,* and *Forbes* all used Zillow content.

Today, Zillow produces two to three different housing reports per week for 350 American cities, with data provided down to the neighborhood level. Zillow sources are quoted as top experts and thought leaders on housing. In the summer of 2013, the White House asked Zillow to partner on a broadcast Q&A streamed on Zillow and Yahoo. Homeowners had the opportunity to ask questions via social media, and President Barack Obama answered them live. Tens of thousands of people participated.

In 2012, Zillow realized there was good news and opportunistic news. The good news was that it was the most-named and most-visited brand in the online real estate category. The opportunistic news was that the category was still very fragmented without a standout national household name. Zillow makes money by charging real estate agents to appear on appropriate pages when a consumer searches a local area. The more people know and use Zillow, the greater the opportunity for the company to sign up real estate agents nationwide.

Zillow knows that people buy homes, on average, every seven years. It wants to attract not just the folks who are looking for a home now (who likely already have a real estate agent), but also people who are thinking about shopping for a home this year, next year, and the year after that. The goal is to embed Zillow in their consciousness so they will start their searches with Zillow first.

That's why in the fall of 2012, Zillow decided to test broadcast TV advertising to generate demand. The company that had been so successful with earned media now wanted to see if paid media would help create awareness above the noise. The impact from the test was highly positive. In 2013, Zillow spent $39 million on TV advertising, with huge returns. In the peak home shopping month of August, traffic was up a whopping 70 percent year over year (YOY). As a result, in 2014, the company spent $75 million in broadcast advertising.

Bohutinsky says Zillow's success is built upon its strength as a trusted content provider. "If we'd started with advertising earlier, we wouldn't have had the same impact," she said. "Now and forever, our base of earned and organic channels will still make up the foundation of our marketing."

What's next? "We want to be the brand in real estate that our children and grandchildren will know. We're still heads down going after the white space for many years," said Bohutinsky. "It's a fun ride!"

Generating Demand by Repurposing Content

Law practice management guru Ed Poll, of LawBiz Management, doesn't have a staff of data analysts generating research reports. However, he *is* an expert at generating relevant content for his audience. Poll works with lawyers who want to improve the profitability of their practices while simultaneously decreasing the stress of managing their business. To do this, he has become a master at leveraging and repurposing content effectively.

Poll has created more material on law practice management than anyone else alive. For the past twenty years, his book *The Attorney and Law Firm Guide to the Business of Law*® has been called the bible for law practice management. The third edition of this guide is just one of three new books Poll published within an eighteen-month period.

Where does the content originate? Poll often starts by creating a short blog post on a topic relevant to the legal community. These posts frequently evolve into articles that are fed to syndicated legal publishers throughout the country. When a topic is too long for an article, Poll turns it into a white paper, booklet, or special report. Sometimes the special reports become books on their own. Poll both self-publishes and works with top legal publishing houses. Often, the same topics are covered in audio or video format or in Poll's weekly newsletter.

Poll finds unusual ways to generate demand by connecting with his target audience. In 2012, he took his silver Airstream trailer on an eleven-thousand-mile cross-country road show. His tour included stops in twenty-one states and presentations to fifteen different bar associations.

The contacts Poll made during the road show were added to his mailing lists, so those people can continue to receive relevant content about law practice management.

How can you leverage the content created throughout your organization? How can you capture, curate, and provide access to the type of content that makes potential prospects and customers consider you an invaluable source of information?

Generating Demand Through Try-and-Buy

Drug dealers may seem like strange role models, but they know how to attract new customers. That first hit of drugs is always free. They want you to try the product and like it. The goal is to get you hooked so you'll keep coming back for more—at a profitable price of course.

While most marketers aren't trying to get customers to build drug habits, they *are* trying to get them to become dependent on what the organization offers. And there's no better way to do that than to offer something for free.

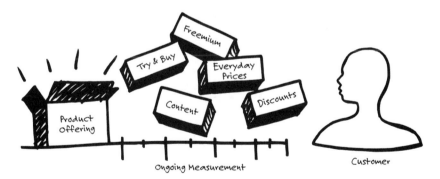

FIGURE 7-1: Demand Generation Bridges the Gap

In today's market, that involves either offering a free trial period or providing a basic service for free but charging for the fully functional product (a model called "freemium").

The free trial period has to be long enough for customers to start using the product and integrate it into their lives. When I recently purchased a new car, Sirius XM gave me a free trial of its satellite radio system. This was not for a week or a month, but for three months. That was just long enough for me to get completely hooked on the product. When the renewal offer came two months into the trial (with a discount for renewing before the trial ended), it was easy for me to say yes.

LinkedIn is an example of a site that offers both free products and paid versions. The basic LinkedIn service is free. If you'd like additional functionality, for conducting more detailed searches on LinkedIn connections or to mine the database to find good job candidates, for example, there are a series of paid options.

LinkedIn is not being altruistic by offering the basic service at no charge to the masses. Part of the allure of its offering is the number of people who participate in the network. The best way to make LinkedIn the "world's largest professional network on the Internet" was to offer profiles at no charge. This critical mass of users, which numbered more than three hundred million worldwide by mid-2014, is what compels sales reps, recruiters, marketers, and others to pay for premium service.[1]

How can your organization effectively use free trials to generate demand? Can you tier your offerings to include both free and paid versions?

Generating Demand Through Outcome-Based Campaigns

BMC Software is a $2.2 billion company that delivers innovative IT management solutions that enable customers to leverage complex technology into extraordinary business performance. In late 2012, Kim DeCarlis joined the company to lead its marketing team, with a goal of making marketing at BMC more strategic and proving that marketing could bring value to the table.

The organization DeCarlis joined was used to producing marketing deliverables but not necessarily thinking strategically. To get above the noise, DeCarlis realized many things would have to change. "The first thing we did was to put aligned objectives into place that were measurable," she said. "That was a mind-set change."

DeCarlis believes it's critical to have a business conversation with the product or sales team upfront. The focus was on the *outcomes* they'd like to see—*not* on the specific deliverables of a marketing campaign. She worked with her team to ask the right open-ended questions so they could understand the desired outcomes. Not every marketing person can handle this. "We had to teach people when to escalate," DeCarlis says. "When there were two really good people trying to solve a problem and it was beyond their capability to get solved, they needed more senior help."

BMC ran an integrated campaign to rebuild the company's reputation in a specific product segment. The marketing team focused on the outcomes desired, as well as on how to measure those outcomes in both the short and long term. Then, said DeCarlis, rather than "peanut-butter the program across the whole world," they ran it in selected geographic areas to see how it would work.

The results? After three months in the market, the campaign outperformed its short-term goals in terms of awareness building and demand generation.

A Dangerous Strategy: Generating Demand Through Discounts

This may sound counterintuitive, but it's usually better to offer something for free, as a try-and-buy incentive, than to offer heavy discounts. As a consumer, I love discounts. Why pay full price for a facial when you can get it for 40 percent off on Groupon or redeem a buy-one-get-one-free offer online?

But as a marketer, I know that discounting has the potential to be downright dangerous. Too many bad things can come from a "more is better" approach to discounting. It's the organizational equivalent of relying on a Costco-sized stash of Halloween candy as the main means of feeding your family. Bouncing from discount to discount is like offering a diet of candy to your customers on an ongoing basis. It does nothing but erode margin and condition your customers to wait for the next deal. It's also harder to maintain market share because customers who buy with discounts tend to have much lower brand loyalty. Now, I love candy as much as the next person (and I truly believe that chocolate is one of the basic food groups!), but it should be part of a relatively balanced diet.

Let's look at the way a perpetual-discount strategy works for Bed, Bath and Beyond, the big-box household goods supplier. The store's blue 20 percent–off coupons are ubiquitous, in both printed and online formats. Furthermore, they don't ever really expire. Store personnel accept these coupons regardless of the printed expiration date. They'll even let you use a whole handful of coupons at one time, to match the number of items you're buying. In effect, what Bed, Bath and Beyond has done is cut its margins by 20 percent. That may work for *that company's* business model, but before following its lead, please consider whether that's the financial direction you want to take for your business!

A little candy after a good meal is a nice treat. Discounts and promotions used judiciously can sweeten a customer's appetite for your offering. But include these in a bigger integrated marketing strategy, where a special really *is* special and not the discount of the week. You don't want your brand to become synonymous with discounts.

It's also important not to cut into your sales by offering customers a discount on something they would have willingly paid full price for anyway. I worked with an organization that gave its field sales team carte blanche to offer special discounts on almost a weekly basis. The team used the special promotions to undercut competitors. But then the competitors turned around and issued their own pricing promotions. You can see where this was going. My client had unwittingly conditioned its customers to wait for the next deal. If it wasn't this week, it was surely going to be the next.

Dynamic Market Leverage Factor 5: Communication

FIGURE 7-2: Dynamic Market Leverage Model—Communication

You can have the best offerings in the world, but if you can't communicate your value to your prospective buyers effectively, you won't be successful in the long run. Effective communications and demand generation programs are usually multifaceted, meaning they have multiple components and touch points. They are also well integrated, fitting together logically, rather than existing as a series of separate programs or events that hit customers in seemingly random fashion.

Whether a prospect or customer interacts with you online or off is not relevant. In today's world, they are likely to see your message in both realms. It is key, however, that the messages customers see are consistent—regardless of where they view them. It's important that your customers receive information from you on a regular basis, and that the messages they receive should reflect who your customers are and where they're likely to go for this kind of information. Meet your customers where they are. Don't make them come to you.

Take the time to carefully consider the content you are putting before your key audiences. What is available to them? How easy is it for them to access this information? An effective content creation and management strategy includes repurposing critical content pieces as appropriate. It also includes culling those pieces of content that are of lower value to your target audience. In some organizations, every group associated with a product is likely to want to get its message to the customer. That's fine when your organization is small. When you have a large, complex organization with multiple product lines, it's important not to overwhelm your customer with "too many": that includes too many messages, too many choices, and too many product offerings that appear to be competitive or at cross-purposes. All that does is raise the noise factor for your customers.

Gone are the days when we thought of digital media strategies and print/broadcast media strategies as distinct entities. Instead, plan for a single integrated media strategy that incorporates the best vehicles for reaching your intended targets. The same applies to a Web presence. A robust Web presence includes a Website that is optimized to meet your marketing objectives. Your Website should help your prospects take the next steps in the purchase and loyalty process. A clear understanding of the customer journey is critical to building a Website that will be optimized for your customers.

Mobile marketing is no longer an option. Assume that your audience will be consuming your content on mobile devices like smartphones and tablets, as well as on traditional PCs. In fact, many people are giving up their desktops and laptops in favor of smart mobile devices exclusively. Your Web presence should be responsive, so that it displays appropriately on mobile devices as well as on browsers on traditional computers. It should include support for those social media channels that are appropriate for your business, which we will discuss in the next chapter.

Generating Demand by Measuring the Right Things

Recently, I served as a judge for the annual Business Marketing Association (BMA) B2 awards, which honor the best examples of business-to-business marketing. Most of the entries I reviewed were quite good. A few were outstanding. What was the difference between good and great? In my opinion, it was not necessarily the creative execution (most were handled well) or the strategy (most seemed to make sense) but the way they measured results.

A few entries had achieved outstanding results, but only a small percentage even measured the right things. In some cases, the metrics themselves were so bland or general that they offered very little guidance as to whether the campaign had been successful. In more than a few instances, the metric supplied was something like, "The client liked the results" or "The vice president seemed happy with the campaign."

Don't get me wrong. I'm as interested in pleasing my clients with my presentations as anyone else. But I want them to be pleased because we improved their condition. It's not about how slick the presentation is or how happy the marketing team or the corporate executives feel when we're done. It's about what changed for the business as a result of the campaign.

What questions should you ask to be sure you're measuring the right things? Start with these:

- Did new customer inquiries increase?
- Did we improve retention of our existing customers, by lowering turnover or churn?
- Did our share of wallet of current customers increase?
- Did we increase revenues?
- Did we build brand? (And, if so, how are we measuring that?)

The entries in the BMA contest certainly don't reflect an isolated situation. In fact, just by including metrics and results as part of the contest criteria, BMA is ahead of most of the pack. I see this situation on a regular basis when talking to marketers across many different industries and organizations.

The flip side of the equation—too many metrics—is no better. Far too often, I see situations where marketers are measuring everything that moves—whether or not these metrics are relevant to moving the needle for the business. This can include the number of clicks on a Web link, the number of followers on Facebook or Twitter, the number of impressions generated, and other such numbers. The problem with most of these "number of" metrics is that they are internal process metrics. They're focused on how well the marketing team executed a particular marketing tactic. They're not external business-related metrics. They don't tell you whether or not the program implemented actually improved your business.

You are what you measure. Be sure to choose the right metrics, focusing on those areas that not only provide useful information, but that your team can actually impact. Knowing a metric went up or down two points isn't relevant to marketers, unless they know what to do with that information. Metrics done well set you free, because the measurement process itself provides a structure within which you can work. The team knows what they are being measured on and why it matters. Metrics provide a means to make midcourse corrections. You can do that long before your marketing rocket is spinning out of control, off to another part of the galaxy far, far away.

Former BMC Software marketing head Kim DeCarlis says she's always believed in measurement. "I think things in marketing absolutely can be measured. The important thing I've put in place with my team is a hierarchy of measurement. Here are the two or three things at the top of the hierarchy that I really care about—that I will report to the executive team and to the board—that tell us marketing is moving the needle."

Beneath those top-level metrics are key performance indicators (KPIs) that indicate something is working. Below that are hundreds of day-to-day metrics that DeCarlis's teams will optimize to get the top-level measurement to where it should be.

Decarlis's focus is on measuring outcomes by implementing initiatives that have impact. That means making trade-offs, cutting resources in one area in order to put additional investment in another. "It's hard to say no," she says. "Marketing is a service organization and we are also people pleasers. It's hard to say. 'No, I can't run that campaign for you—I can't do that product launch the way you'd like it to be done.'"

The right metrics provide a means for marketing organizations to show their value to the rest of the organization in a concrete way that the organization can truly understand. That helps both marketers and executives justify the investment the organization is making in marketing.

Dynamic Market Leverage Factor 6: Operations

FIGURE 7-3: Dynamic Market Leverage Model—Operations

It's sometimes hard to consider day-to-day operations and infrastructure as a strategic part of a marketing function, yet it is here that many well-intentioned efforts fall by the wayside. A successful organization will look at operations from a strategic perspective, deploying and using key analytic tools to track and evaluate marketing initiatives. An effective marketing team ensures that goals and objectives are supported by the correct key performance indicators and metrics, and that these metrics are tracked and reviewed regularly. Information on the effectiveness of marketing initiatives should be communicated on an ongoing basis through easy-to-comprehend dashboards.

Marketing automation is critical to today's successful marketing organization. It's important to have the right tools available to streamline management and delivery of campaigns and programs. According to Forrester Research, 61 percent of B2B marketing executives surveyed expected the ratio of money spent on technology versus marketing programs to increase in 2014.[2]

All marketing today is global, whether we want it to be or not. Processes should be in place to ensure that marketing initiatives are global in nature, with the ability to localize as appropriate within various territories or geographies.

Finally, high-achieving marketing organizations that stand out above the noise actively seek out and adopt best practices from other organizations. They choose those elements that will work for them and adapt them to the requirements of their particular business.

PART III

Striking the Right Chord

8

Closing the Sale: How Marketing and Sales Can Work in Harmony

My first paying job was with the circus. No, I wasn't a lion tamer or a trapeze artist. My job was more mundane, but it taught me quite a bit about business…and about sales. Every spring during Easter break, the Ringling Bros. and Barnum & Bailey Circus came to my town in northeastern Pennsylvania. Because it was a vacation week, I signed up to work as a food vendor.

I was assigned to sell one of the most popular products, snow cones. A tray of snow cones came pre-configured with four flavors. Orange and cherry were crowd-pleasers, but grape and root beer were not popular. However, you couldn't get a new tray of product until you'd sold everything on your old one.

I realized that there were two ways to get the product to customers. I could stand on the ground and pass snow cones up to buyers in the crowd. That was how most of the other vendors operated. Or I could take the time to climb up among the spectators and deliver the goods directly.

When I made the time and effort to climb up to my customers, invariably someone would look at me standing there and say, "Gee, Gladys, here's the girl with the snow cones. Why don't we get a couple while she's standing here? Who knows how long it will be until someone else bothers to come our way!" Even when the only cones I had left were grape or, heaven forbid, the highly disliked root beer, the fact that I was standing right in front of them led my customers to override their hesitance and make the purchase.

By the third day, I had nearly doubled my sales. By the end of the week, I was one of the star vendors. And, inadvertently, I had my first lesson on how interacting with customers affects the sales process.

Where Does Marketing Stop and Selling Begin?

It may be hard for younger readers to believe, but there was a time when consumers were content to be sold *to*. People watched and listened to just a few mass media channels and publications. Consumers used what they learned via those channels to make decisions when they went to a physical store to make a purchase.

This was before the Internet was accessible to the masses and before search engines could be used to research a product or service instantly. It took a *lot* of time to go around asking friends, colleagues, or other purchasers what they thought about a brand or product. Going "viral" meant the onset of a bad illness, something to be avoided at all costs.

In that world, sales teams provided a clear value to the customer. Customers relied on sales representatives, whether in a store or an office, to be highly knowledgeable about the products they were selling. Typically, the selling organization was the consumer's primary source of product information. Buyers expected a salesperson to be able to quickly ascertain their needs as customers and to help them determine which product was most appropriate. And they expected a sales rep to guide them through the whole sales process, from start to finish.

Marketing's role in this scenario was twofold. First, it helped generate awareness and demand for the products offered. Second, it created compelling marketing materials that would attract attention and convince customers to listen to sales pitches.

Something Sold, Something New

Many years ago, a sales manager told me that all sales forces are by nature "coin-operated." If you give salespeople something to sell and tell them their compensation will be based on selling that product, then that's what they'll sell. Period.

But consumers today are no longer passive recipients in the sales process. They're in the driver's seat. As such, they define how, where, and when they will participate in the purchase of goods and services. And they certainly aren't going to be persuaded by a sales rep pushing the product that gives him a bigger commission check. This puts sales reps into uncharted waters. Where do they fit? How do they add value?

It also causes consternation for the marketers who support them. Producing the same old marketing materials of yesteryear isn't going to cut it when the roles of the customer and the sales rep have changed so dramatically. As marketers, we need to understand how to be better partners to the sales team. That means we need to understand the challenges sales reps face in today's ultra-noisy business environment.

Different Results from a New Mind-Set

What makes a successful salesperson? In his recent bestseller, *To Sell Is Human,* author Dan Pink tells us we're all in sales—whether we have the word "sales" in our titles or not. Just by being human, he says, we have "a selling instinct, which means that anyone can master the basics of moving others."[1]

If you don't think that makes sense, consider that there's probably no better salesperson than your young child when some new object of desire catches his eye. Your spouse or significant other is probably a close second in this regard. Yet if it's true that everyone has a salesperson inside, why are some organizations much better at selling products and services than others? Is it because they hire better sales reps? Do they have better products? Or does it have something to do with their marketing?

In her book *Selling with Noble Purpose,* Lisa McLeod says a key difference is whether an organization has noble purpose. Does that organization truly want to make a difference in the lives of its customers? [2]

McLeod says organizations *without* noble purpose focus on trying to sell as many of their products or services as they possibly can. Their marketing materials tend to be feature oriented, or they may talk in a generic way about benefits. Their driving force: how can we sell more of whatever product or service our organization is offering?

Organizations *with* noble purpose ask how they can improve life for their customers. *Their* marketing materials are very different. These materials include concrete, emotive descriptions of how customers' lives have been improved. McLeod says this nuance in thinking is the difference between boring marketing campaigns and those that resonate with customers.

Noble purpose-driven marketing starts with a great value proposition. McLeod says that many value propositions are long-winded affairs that are product-centric rather than customer-centric. She recommends starting with a noble purpose statement that breaks down the value proposition into solid examples of what customers have done with your product or service.

From there, marketing and sales teams can work together to create a compelling value proposition that incorporates the noble purpose concept. McLeod warns against letting the idea of noble purpose degenerate into a tag line. She notes that in some companies, salespeople just repeat marketing tag lines like mantras, which is not usually effective.

Sales reps really need to know their content—the features and benefits of what they sell—so that they can have an authentic conversation with the customer. Applying noble purpose to messaging is the easy part. Getting marketing and salespeople to work amicably together is often a challenge.

Are We Harmonizing or Shouting at Each Other?

If sales and marketing teams have similar goals, why do they often find themselves so at odds? The sibling rivalry between sales and marketing probably goes back to the first organization that had both a sales rep and a marketing person. It likely wasn't long after farmers first brought their wares to market thousands of years ago that someone said, "Gee, I'm better at getting our milk and butter packaged for Wednesday's market. You're better at handling the discussions with the people who want to trade their products for ours. Let's divide up the responsibilities and each handle what we do best." From there, the sales and marketing twins were born.

And, as often happens with siblings, the two have regularly agreed to disagree on how they work together ever since. This reminds me of the story about a hotel in the Catskills. One old lady says to another, "I hate that place! The food is terrible, the menu choices are limited, and everything is overcooked!" The second woman replies, "Yes. And such small portions, too!"

Sales often thinks the marketing team just throws stuff over the wall: their attitude seems to be, "It's not right. You're not moving fast enough. But please can we get more?" Look at the issue from the sales perspective. They tend to be in front of difficult customers, day after day. Those ungrateful marketing people just don't understand what it's like to be on the front lines and not have the right ammunition to win. From marketing's point of view, it's not clear why those ungrateful salespeople don't appreciate all the hard work the marketing team does for them.

So sales thinks *marketing* just wants them to execute against a marketing plan that *marketing* insists sales should follow. While marketing thinks *sales* just wants them to execute against a set of deliverables that *sales* has demanded from marketing. See a pattern here? Both sides are focused on executing in their own siloed way. They're not trying to harmonize together to get above the noise.

Organizations that have gotten beyond this dynamic have changed the way marketing and salespeople approach each other. Rather than looking for whom to blame, they have formed a partnership in which they work together to understand how best to approach customers.

One of the most effective ways I've found to get sales and marketing working in sync is to put marketing people on the sales team. Have them participate in sales calls. Let them sit quietly and watch what customers say and do in real-life situations. (It's extremely valuable for other organizational functions, such as R&D, to do this as well.) The marketing team members who have been out in the field come back with a new understanding of what customers want and what the sales team needs. The sales team appreciates that the folks from headquarters have come out to see what happens in the field.

The reverse is also true. It's helpful to involve the sales team in the marketing process. This brings the sales perspective into the marketing effort, and it helps sales understand what's involved in creating marketing initiatives.

How else can marketing be a more effective partner to sales? Lisa McLeod says marketers need to understand there's a big difference between marketing materials that stand alone and those that can be effectively used by a sales force in a customer call.

FIGURE 8-1: Sales–Marketing Alignment

Marketers are moving away from one-size-fits-all marketing campaigns to more customizable, personalized communications. McLeod says marketers need to understand that sales tools should be customizable as well. While the marketing department will go to great lengths to identify competitive differentiators, it's important to leave enough room for sales reps to have open, interactive conversations with prospective customers, so they can move the sales process forward.

Don't Confuse Selling with Installing

At Sun Microsystems, our sales reps would often sell a customer the solution they thought the customer wanted. The trouble was that it was not necessarily the system the customer support team was prepared to show up and install. That disconnect between expectations and reality would get us into trouble if we weren't prepared to address it head on. "Don't confuse selling with installing" was an important lesson I've carried with me since then. It's easy to sell the promise of what can be. It's not so easy to implement something that fulfills that promise in the light of day and on an ongoing basis.

This idea is not limited to technology products. In the political arena in 2008, a little-known presidential candidate named Barack Obama sold an eager American public on a concept they were ready to embrace: change you can believe in.

The problem is that once elected president, Mr. Obama discovered that campaigning for office is very different from governing a country of the size and complexity of the United States. Talking about change is one thing. Having the will, discipline, and bipartisan political support to actually implement it is something else altogether.

Confusing selling with installing is one reason marketing and sales often find themselves at odds. Marketing produces the messaging and campaigns that give the sales team the air cover they need to sell products and services. But sales is an emotional process. As consultant Alan Weiss says, logic makes people think but emotion makes them act.

It's important that sales, marketing, and support teams work together to ensure that the messages they are driving translate into a product or service that can actually be delivered. At the end of the day, the customer has to be satisfied with what is actually "installed," not the idealistic solution they originally thought they were buying.

In a recent *Harvard Business Review* article, Aditya Joshi and Eduardo Gimenez talk about a global technology company that found its sales reps were "spending an average of nearly one day a week digging around in the company's systems to find or develop what they felt they needed, instead of spending time with customers."[3] By clarifying roles and the decision-making process, this organization was able to move to a model where collateral materials meet the needs of reps, while maintaining consistency with marketing brand guidelines. And the organization's sales reps can devote more time to selling.[4]

Salespeople are entering the buying process much later than in previous years. According to marketing automation provider Marketo, "Seventy percent of the buying process in a complex sale is already complete before a potential customer is ready to engage with a sales person."[5] So, by the time a customer contacts a salesperson, she's already formed a perception of what she wants based on information she found online, discussions with friends and colleagues, or perhaps even shopping the competition. That means sales reps need to be much more effective at discerning a customer's true objectives, and they need to do it quickly. It also means marketing needs to adapt to give sales reps the tools they need to be successful in today's noisy world.

Lisa McLeod says there are several ways marketing teams can more effectively help salespeople. First, marketing can provide better-quality market analysis and information about the market environment in which the company competes. Marketing can also provide sales reps with the subject matter expertise they need to ask better questions. And marketing can create an online experience that gets customers on the right track.

Alliances: Who's on Whose Side?

Sometimes the best salespeople you can put on your team aren't on your team at all—they're employees of someone else. Partnerships and alliances are a key way for organizations to extend their reach in the marketplace. Partners are more than just additional feet on the street. They can help provide a level of credibility, market reach, and position that organizations can't get on their own, according to Norma Watenpaugh, president of Phoenix Consulting Group and a global board member of the Association of Strategic Alliance Professionals (ASAP).

Watenpaugh notes that Sun Microsystems' move from the technical workstation space to more commercial computing required a different type of sales force. Systems integrators knew many of these vertical markets much better than Sun did. They had more than just reputation, they also had backgrounds in applications, professional services, and other areas that customers expected from a systems provider.

The goal is to make 1+1 = 3. Together, an organization and its partners create new value for customers. The organization wins. The partners win. Most importantly, the customers win, too.

Not all alliances are the same, says Watenpaugh. Some are focused on providing the technology or complementary functionality required to complete a product or service for a specific market. Others focus on integrating multiple products into a full turnkey solution for the end customer. Still others are focused on helping to get a product to market.

As head of the Google Apps Global Partner Program, Jim Chow was responsible for the overall Apps partner business and success of more than ten thousand apps resellers worldwide. He says Google thinks of partners as extensions of the Google team. The company's goal is to integrate partners into the Google ecosystems as much as possible, so that partners can work from a position of strength when they sell Google for Work products to their customers.

To have this kind of synchronicity, it's important that the marketing team look at what it is creating through the eyes of the partner. That means making sure marketing materials and campaigns are all channel-ready. They should be easily adopted and adaptable by channel and alliance partners.

There's a big difference between marketing *to* a partner (recruiting the partner to be on your team and keeping them informed about new product offerings and selling opportunities) and marketing *through* a partner (to reach the partner's customers). To get above the noise when marketing *through* a partner, you'll need to work together to understand the partner's customers. Ask all the same questions you'd ask about your own customers. Who are they? What motivates them? How can we work together to improve their situation? Together, you'll need to craft a marketing approach that incorporates the partner's strengths with the solutions your organization provides. Ideally, the customer should see the alliance as offering much more value than either party could provide separately.

Channeling a New Force

Erna Arnesen is the vice president of global channel and partner marketing at Plantronics, a leading supplier of audio communications products for businesses and consumers. For fifty years, Plantronics headsets have been used by everyone from pilots, astronauts, and 911 emergency workers to employees at every single company in the Fortune 100.

Arnesen's job is to grow the channel for Plantronics' enterprise products—those corded or wireless headsets used to boost employee productivity within corporations. Her team's responsibility is in supporting, enabling, and incentivizing those channel partners that sell Plantronics products to enterprise customers.

Arnesen says that to get above the noise, she makes sure her team is focused on how they can offer additional value to their channel partners. She says that, while it's important for a channel marketing program to have strong demand generation, deal registration, and promotional reward programs, it's critical to set the strategic direction first.

Channel marketing groups like Arnesen's are often funded through the sales budget, which means it's critical that they align closely with the sales team. At Plantronics, the channel marketing team is constantly refining how they help partners go to market. It's not just marketing *to* channel partners, but also *through* them and *with* them. Plantronics works to use its resources as effectively as possible to support its channel partners, including creating demand and motivating and rewarding partners that perform.

There's always more to do. Arnesen says she sees great opportunities to build upon a solid partner program and to continue to move the needle for Plantronics in terms of generating incremental revenue through channel partners. How well does this work? Plantronics' partners regularly give the company high marks as one of their preferred partners. And that's something the company loves to hear.

Dynamic Market Leverage Factor 7: Sales Channels

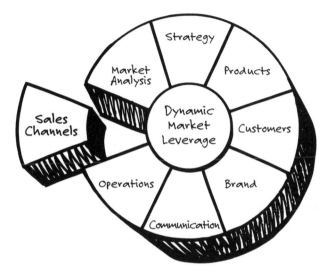

FIGURE 8-2: Dynamic Market Leverage Model—Sales

If marketing opens the door to customers, it is sales that closes the process—through a captive sales force, independent representatives, or sales channels, partners, and alliances. Marketing's role is to support the needs of both direct field sales and indirect channels by providing the messaging, branding, and marketing materials that help expedite the sales process.

This means involving sales in the process, so the marketing team understands how products and services are sold, where support is required, and what type of marketing materials will be most effective. It means listening to what sales reps say they are encountering on the ground on a daily basis. It means using this intelligence to create helpful tools such as reference stories, testimonials, and use cases. And it means having these available in a wide variety of formats—including text, audio, and video.

It's important that you communicate on an ongoing basis with your sales force and channels so that they understand the messaging and positioning of each of your organization's offerings. It means keeping your field force up to date with what your competitors are saying and

doing, and guiding them to ammunition when required for specific customer situations.

Provide ongoing training to your sales teams to ensure that new and
existing partners are up to speed on products, services, and support.
Ensure that all of your communications are channel-ready and appropriate for use by partners as well as by your direct sales force.

You'll need to do more than just capturing prospect and customer
information from CRM tools, like Salesforce.com. You'll need to actually
analyze and use the information to develop and deploy the best possible
marketing initiatives to the best possible prospects.

Look at sales and channels as your partner—a conduit to success—
and harmonize with them to get the results you need to get above the
noise.

Best Practices in Making Alliances Work Effectively

Norma Watenpaugh of Phoenix Consulting Group (Phoenix CG) has
been leading the charge to get organizations to build strategic advantage
through alliances. Together with the Association for Strategic Alliance
Professionals (ASAP), Phoenix CG has conducted ongoing research on
best practices in high-performing technology alliances.

The findings of the research indicate that high performers put a much
higher priority on innovation compared with other organizations. These
higher-performing organizations take a more strategic view in how they
can leverage alliances to drive new streams of revenue.

When it comes to go-to-market strategies (an area near and dear to
my heart), the higher-performing organizations were investing from 1 to
3 percent of their projected revenue into marketing with their partners.
They dedicated marketing dollars to partner marketing, and they made
sure to have a budget allocated to partner marketing for each fiscal year.
Even if the amount was small, having a predetermined budget allowed
both sides to know what they could and couldn't do.

Phoenix found best-in-class organizations focused strongly on metrics across the entire cycle of development—not just in terms of sales pipelines. They developed a full set of measurements to evaluate the success of the alliance from end to end, including an assessment of the alliance's effectiveness in creating and driving demand.

The bottom line: those organizations that are more successful in leveraging alliances take a more strategic view. They see strong alliance partnerships as yet another way they can rise above the noise in the marketplace. Perhaps more importantly, they strategically create competitive advantage through greater customer value, taking additional market share.

9

The Big Deal About Big Data

Several months after buying a new house, I realized I needed to change the water filter on my refrigerator. Rather than taking the time to drive to the store, I decided to order a new filter online. Numerous sites offered the correct filter, including the appliance manufacturer's Website and several online appliance stores. Before ordering, I thought I'd check to see if the item was available from Amazon.com. Lo and behold, not only was the filter available at a lower price, but because I subscribe to Amazon Prime, there was no charge for shipping.

These water filters need to be replaced twice a year, but I'm not likely to remember to do it until my fridge flashes the "change the filter" light. Amazon allowed me to set up an automatic shipment of filters every six months. I signed up for this option and promptly forgot about it. Six months later, just as I was wondering when I needed to order a new water filter, Amazon delivered a box with the filter inside to my doorstep. This required absolutely no effort from me. Now that's helpful.

How does the company do this? By leveraging Big Data. Amazon captures and analyzes data on billions and billions of transactions to build profiles of customers and to understand how and where Amazon can help them—even before they know they need help.

The question is, how can we as marketers use Big Data to help our organizations stand out above the noise? Let's look at how Big Data can lead to big insights for marketers, as well as how the relationship of the CMO to the CIO changes in a Big Data–driven world. We'll also examine what's quickly becoming the new digital divide.

Data, Data Everywhere

More data has been produced in the last few years than in the entire history of humankind up to 2005. Market research firm Forrester says that in 2015, there will be one trillion connected objects and devices generating 2.5 billion gigabytes of data *every day*. Eighty percent of this data will be unstructured, meaning it's not organized in a preconfigured manner, like in a relational database.[1]

Today's technology can capture and analyze these huge sets of raw data quickly and efficiently so the information can inform real-time decision making. The result is what's now called Big Data. Big Data gives marketers the ability to understand patterns of customer behavior that were not previously apparent, and to predict with reasonable accuracy which customer will take which steps next. However, there's also the potential we'll get lost in the details. There's so much tantalizing stuff to look at. So much data. So much analysis that can be done. So many possible actions to take.

Our friends from Amazon are leveraging Big Data big time. On top of the largest selection of books in the world, the company added a broad selection of other products, from office supplies to pet products to those water filters that magically appear on my doorstep.

Amazon introduced second-day, no-effort-required shipping through its Prime program. Then it offered Prime customers the ability to stream video content at no extra charge. It's also added lockers that allow customers to pick up products the same day they place the order. And Amazon is reportedly considering building a fleet of drones so it can offer an unmanned delivery option.

All pretty impressive stuff, but consider where Amazon is going next: patenting a predictive customer algorithm. That's right. Amazon has a patent pending on technology that will allow the company to look at your past buying behavior, predict what you are likely to order next, and send the items to you…before you even indicate you're interested in them! Amazon has amazing confidence in this algorithm. If the prediction is wrong and you really don't want an item, instead of incurring the cost to have you send it back, they'll let you keep it.

Rather than just ship me my next water filter, Amazon will soon be able to say, "Since you've already bought water filters and various other products from us, we're going to send you something you've never bought before but we think you'll use. And we'll send it before you even know you need it or want it." Wow.

Amanda Setili, author of *The Agility Advantage: How to Identify and Act On Opportunities in a Fast-Changing World,* notes that Big Data allows organizations to see when changes first start in the market, so that they can jump on trends faster. It allows companies to identify niche segments that until now were not easily noticed. They can decide to cater to these segments or just keep an eye on them to see if they're growing.

All this can happen in real time. For example, says Setili, a company can use sensor data embedded in a product to monitor how the product is being used and how it is faring in the world. This means the company can send a customized message to a user before it's apparent that there's a problem. Think about a car that told you before a timing belt broke or a refrigerator that let you know it was about to fail before it destroyed a week's worth of perishable groceries.

The San Francisco 49ers are using Big Data to build "fan engagement" with a program called Faithful 49. Users earn points by interacting with the team and its sponsors. Prizes include discounts on jerseys or tickets to sold-out games at the team's brand new Levi's Stadium. The 49ers will be incorporating gamification to spur competition among fans with features like a real-time public leader board. The idea is to encourage fans to keep participating and share data. A fan who posts about a Colin Kaepernick touchdown pass might receive a promotional offer for a Kaepernick jersey, for example.[2]

How could your organization leverage Big Data? How could you use it to build stronger relationships with your customers? How would you change the way you build demand-generation campaigns?

Let's look at what insights from Big Data did for Xbox Live.

Xbox Live: Big Data Informs Marketing Decisions

It's one thing to have access to data. It's quite another to understand what the data means and how to leverage it to get above the noise. Craig Davison, former senior director of marketing at Microsoft, had been heading up marketing for the company's Xbox games in 2007 when he moved to the Xbox Live group.

At that time Xbox Live, an online gaming service launched in 2002, had about eighteen million members, half of whom were paid subscribers. Video game marketing was somewhat like marketing Hollywood films. The goal was to build hype, awareness, and buzz way in advance of a game's launch. Selling an online gaming service was significantly different—it was much more like subscription model marketing, where the goal is to acquire, retain, and monetize members. That meant identifying the barriers that might prevent consumers from joining the service or renewing their subscriptions. It also meant finding better ways to enable customers to buy the digital items sold on the service—from avatar clothing to actual games.

Davison and his team became immersed in key performance indicators and real-time feedback. They had more data and business insights than they knew what to do with. So the team tried to ask key questions: What's the probability of someone making a purchase if we give them something free? What if we give them enough credits to buy a game so they can just get started? Do we have any data to show that this will actually work? And the problem was—they didn't.

In retrospect, Davison says, the mistake was thinking all they needed was data. "What we forgot is that you needed people to do nothing except acquire that data and then translate the data into insights. It was deeply personal and very painful, because people thought, if I'm not capable of taking this data and translating it into an insight, I'm out of a job." That wasn't the case. The Xbox Live team needed people who could work with the data *and* they needed people who could be creative and produce marketing campaigns.

"Suddenly you became partners with the data and analytics folks who were bringing that data to you. They were helping you develop the campaign, so that as you created it, everything you did was in turn measurable," Davison says. "But everyone and their mother had an idea on what the data meant, and what the insights should be. It was a lot of people running into each other and it was chaos."

What the team learned was that social media weren't driving Xbox Live subscriptions. The Website wasn't driving subscriptions. Offers in physical game boxes weren't driving subscriptions. Neither were all of the marketing campaigns the team tried: digital, display advertising, re-targeting, direct mail, etc. What *did* drive subscriptions was what was on the Xbox Live interface itself—the dashboard menu that controlled what users could do with the service.

That meant the team dialed down the external media campaigns and focused instead on how to improve the user experience with the Xbox Live dashboard. They created technology that allowed users to renew online, within the product. They experimented with making different offers at different times of day and associated with different games.

Over time, the team learned that the number-one thing that drove customer acquisition of the Xbox Live service was a game launch. So if a new version of a game like *Call of Duty* launched, Microsoft timed marketing offers to coincide with the launch of that game.

Hard-core gamers hate advertising. So instead of ads, the Xbox Live team created additional content in the form of extra uniforms, guns, and other items that gamers *did* find interesting. This created a lucrative source of revenue for game developers and incented them to create a rich online experience for their users.

Davison said understanding the insights from the Xbox Live subscriber data was a massive learning for the team. Once they realized game content drove demand, and that interactions happened at the dashboard level, they were able to put marketing resources where they really mattered. "It came down to content and value proposition," said Davison. "If you had an amazing online game experience with the right audience and the right game genre, then it absolutely would work. And if you didn't, it wouldn't."

Testing . . . 1, 2, 3

One of the big benefits of the new data-driven world is that it's fairly straightforward to test different marketing alternatives to see which is most effective. The Web allows easy AB testing, where we can try multiple approaches to see which performs better, A or B. Marketers are now able to fine-tune their campaigns to optimize messages, delivery mechanisms, e-mail headers, and even time of day of delivery in near real time.

We're able to pilot marketing initiatives at a low cost and conduct beta tests on a small but reliable scale. This allows us as marketers to figure out what works and what needs to be changed, and it keeps costs down. Then we are able to pivot and make changes in real time.

Deeper and Broader at the Same Time

One of the advantages of the new Big Data environment is that it allows us to know more, potentially do less, and yet be more effective. How is this possible? Consider this:

- Big Data allows marketers to know *more* about customers—not just who they are, but what they do and when they do it.
- We can know *more* about the context in which customers and prospects are likely to interact with us.
- We know *more* about how these people are likely to connect—with an organization, a brand, and each other.
- We know *more* about many more people.
- We can analyze data *more* deeply.
- We can collect *more* data.
- We are able to *more* accurately predict behavior, based on data.
- We can *more* effectively track behavior—in a time frame that lets us react quickly and make timely changes.

How does data allow us to do less?

- We can spend *less* time reacting to results, good or bad, from earlier marketing efforts.
- We can do *less* generic mass marketing…because we will be personalizing marketing campaigns.
- We can spend *less* money on wasted marketing efforts.

Ask your marketing team how they will take the new insights they're learning and apply these to building more effective marketing campaigns. Where will you put additional resources? Where will you do less? Where can you make a bigger impact to get above the noise?

Analysts Are Important; Decision Makers Are Paramount

It's becoming obvious that to be successful, today's marketing teams need people who understand and can interpret data. Data science is important, no matter how large or small your organization and how big your budget. But it's not enough. Marketers start by collecting and analyzing data. The number of tools available for marketing and sales data analysis grows on nearly a daily basis. As a marketer, you need to be able to choose the right analytics to start. Then you'll need to master the tools, create metrics, and produce and distribute useful reports.

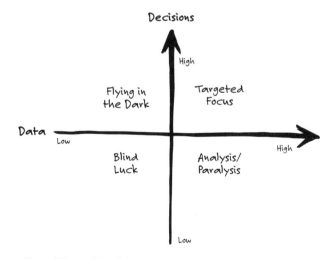

FIGURE 9-1: Data Versus Decisions

However, marketing teams that get above the noise do more than this. They also have people with big-picture capability who understand how to use these new insights to improve decision making. They don't abdicate responsibility for major marketing decisions, deferring to the analysts.

At the end of the day, it's not how big the data is that matters. It's the business insights gained and the decisions made *because* that data is available. It's about how an organization *uses* that data to help its customers.

Sharing Data Insights to Assist Customers

Manheim is the leading provider of vehicle remarketing services. In 1945, the company ran its first wholesale vehicle auction with just three vehicles down one auction lane. Today, Manheim handles nearly seven million used vehicles per year, facilitating transactions representing more than $46 billion in value. The company brings together qualified sellers and volume buyers of used vehicles, including automotive dealerships, banks, car rental agencies, car manufacturers, and government agencies. Manheim offers both in-person and online vehicle marketplaces, as well as financing and transportation options.

According to Stephen Smith, senior director, customer marketing, the company acts as a leading source of used vehicle information that helps the industry and its customers make informed decisions.

How does Manheim use data to stand out above the noise? Smith says the company's goal is to improve the experience for customers. This is not just in terms of the way it manages transactions, but also the information Manheim provides to customers and the way it serves dealers as a business partner. "One of the key things we're trying to do is to grow the business by using our comprehensive auction data to help customers make more informed business decisions, while tailoring our offerings to them," said Smith.

As Manheim moves to take its relationship with customers to a new level, it's finding new skill sets are needed in the organization. "This is a different way to go to market, a different way of doing marketing. In the past, our industry was very locally based, so a lot of the decisions that were made and the marketing programs developed were local in nature, and very event driven," says Smith.

He notes that what's been effective in the past is not what will work in the new world. "How you use data, how you use technology tools and deploy them—these are different skill sets. We're learning as we go along how to bring that to life in the company." Smith notes that Manheim wants to build an organization around people who can translate data into actionable insights: "The fortuitous thing for us is that we already had data analysis in place within marketing. We have some highly skilled data analysts, so we are further ahead than a lot of organizations might be if they were just starting on this journey. But we do have some gaps. How do we take that data, derive insights from it, and put it in the hands of people who are going to build engagement programs and campaigns?" For Manheim, the real measure of success is whether the right customers are coming to Manheim sales, whether online or in-lane (the physical auctions).

Another area of differentiation for Manheim is in collaborating with its sister companies within Cox Automotive: NextGear Capital, AutoTrader, Ready Auto Transport, and Kelley Blue Book. For example, Manheim can provide insights using AutoTrader research to gain enhanced understanding into what common customers across the two companies might require. It also works closely with NextGear Capital, the world's leading independent inventory finance company, to provide wholesale vehicle financing, also known as floor planning, to independent dealers. But leveraging *all* of the assets of Cox Automotive can be a game changer. Smith says:

This has the potential to fundamentally reshape what our value proposition is for our customer. Until now, it's always been about the transaction. The vision for us is that the role we play in a new, more virtual environment will change. We can be a tremendous partner to our customers by sharing insights and research that we have to help them make smarter decisions in their transactions and the way that they conduct business. That can apply to customers who want to transport vehicles, to acquire vehicles, to sell vehicles in the wholesale marketplace, to finance their inventory, or some other service that we provide.

Smith notes that one of the new realities is that it's not possible to always have a comprehensive picture of how everything fits together. "You can't just say, 'Here's the strategy, here's the three-year plan, let's put a structure in place.' You learn new information all the time. You have strategy, but also a lot of flexibility and the ability to respond quickly. You never have all the answers."

Strange Big Data Bedfellows: CMOs and CIOs

In the past, corporate marketing and IT groups usually went their own ways. Marketing was responsible for branding and demand generation. The IT group was responsible for mission-critical corporate data systems. For the most part, they didn't need to interact that closely. But today, when data is an integral part of marketing strategy, CMOs find they need to work more closely with their CIO brethren.

In 2012, market research firm Gartner predicted that by 2017, CMOs will spend more on IT than their counterpart CIOs. At the time, it seemed like an outrageous statement. However, the closer we get to 2017, the more it looks like Gartner may be right.[3]

Meg Bear is the group vice president, social cloud at Oracle, responsible for the social relationship management product suite that brings the power of social to the enterprise. Her group produces Oracle's social media management tools for listening, engagement, marketing, and insight.

Bear says one of the biggest issues between CIOs and CMOs is the way they look at time frames. The CIO is used to event horizons that span years and even decades. The CMO, on the other hand, is measured on campaigns that last for a much shorter time frame. By recognizing these different perspectives up front, the two sides can forge a more effective working relationship.

Looking at this difference from the CIO perspective can help a CMO stand out above the noise. For example, Bear says CIOs know how to build business cases for a technology solution. They're often enthusiastic to help innovate inside an organization. CMOs know how to get results very quickly—which is like a breath of fresh air for the CIO, who often has to wait several years to show results from an infrastructure project.

Bear recommends finding a path to commonality. "Instead of saying, 'We can't do anything till we can do the perfect thing,' say, 'This is what we can do today to meet this particular goal and this is how we will iterate on that to make something sustainable longer term.'"

Will marketers need a stronger IT education in the future? Bear says all of our lives are more technical. Certainly, it's important that CMOs are comfortable in a digital world. They should also be comfortable with data analysis and the opportunities that come from using data. Data analysts and data scientists should be part of today's marketing team. However, Bear says marketers might consider partnering with IT instead of engaging outside expertise to evaluate technology acquisition. Her recommendation: understand your core needs and the additional needs you expect to have. "Make sure you have a technology partner that helps you with interoperability in a way that protects you from that being your problem as a marketer," she advises.

The Looming Digital Divide

It used to be that the digital divide was about who had technology and who didn't. In the future, it is likely to take on a different definition: who uses data effectively and who doesn't.

Access to good data, tools, and processes to analyze data appropriately will be the minimum requirements for successful entry into a market. However, the ability to gain appropriate insights from those analyses and to effectively use those results will separate those who stand above the noise from those who are lost in the crowd.

Knowing which data to collect is a key starting point. Data must be collected from high-quality sources, and it must be reproducible. As Amy Bohutinsky noted, Zillow would not have gotten traction had it not been able to provide solid data on the real estate market to its users.

Focusing on old-style marketing objectives without understanding how this new digital divide changes the game is another issue. Those who are not able to keep up in this game will be left in the dust. They'll be guessing at what their customers have done and what they're likely to do. Their competitors will be working from a position of strength by relying on knowledge of customers' past behavior and projections about potential future actions.

It's also about quick response time. Market leaders will be able to respond much faster as well as much more knowledgeably. Forrester Research says firms will have to act at the speed of the customer, which is the speed that will "satisfy the customers' need for immediate information, product, or service delivery."[4] This speed should be "as near to real time as possible, as timing becomes increasingly critical to an enhanced customer experience."[5]

This can't be done piecemeal. You can't be successful without understanding *all* of your customer data. The scary part is that most organizations are collecting at least a good part of this data—but they're not necessarily using it. Useful data may be spread across disparate systems that don't talk to each other. In some cases, data is still being collected in silos across the organization and not shared among various groups or divisions.

Your competitors are likely working hard to use data as a competitive advantage. Can you afford to let them leapfrog your organization? Look for hidden repositories of data. A great place to start is with those employees who interact with customers on a regular basis, as we'll see in the next chapter.

Dynamic Market Leverage Factor 8: Market Analysis

FIGURE 9-2: Dynamic Market Leverage Model—Market Analysis

The better you understand your customers' and prospects' current situations, the better you can be at providing solutions they are likely to embrace. Knowing about your competition gives you an advantage, too.

Marketers have traditionally looked for customer input into product offerings. However, it's important to be aware that what customers tell you they need is only part of the equation. Customers didn't tell Steve Jobs they needed iPods or iTunes. Jobs was smart enough to look at the technology music listeners were using and ponder the possibilities with a whole new metaphor for personal music usage, by creating iTunes, an online digital music library, and making the iPod the way to access this new library.

Looking for unmet needs is critical step, but it's important not to do this in a vacuum. Successful organizations analyze external forces. They ask what their competition is doing and what they are likely to do in the future. They look at how the economic situation might impact customers. And they use Big Data to uncover trends that may change the way customers behave.

This kind of analysis helps to identify which new markets or industries might be most attractive for future growth. It's important to put together plans and processes to capture high-potential new markets. What can be applied from our existing market position? What's different in new markets? Where are there unique differences that must be specifically addressed?

Underlying all of this is the need for clean, quality customer and market data as the core for market analysis efforts. It sounds straightforward, but too often organizations use the data that is readily available to them without allowing for the fact that it may be out of date, inaccurate, or incomplete. Big Data doesn't necessarily mean clean data. Garbage in is still garbage out. Starting from an inaccurate or false premise will lead you down the wrong path, and it wastes precious time and resources.

Understanding your products, your customers, and your markets is necessary to get above the noise, but it's not sufficient. The brand you painstakingly develop and the communications you carefully craft are put in the hands of a group that often gets little attention from those who develop marketing strategy: employees. Let's look at the key role employees play in this process.

10

How Employees Raise the Volume

Airlines are notorious for poor customer service, from losing baggage to canceling flights to treating passengers as necessary annoyances. How unusual is it, then, to hear the story of a passenger who had such a positive experience on a flight that she staged a public display of thanks in an airport terminal.

Southwest Airlines passenger Shawna Suckow, an author, walked off a flight to Minneapolis in mid-2013 and left behind her laptop, which stored the only copy of her new book's nearly completed manuscript. By the time she realized what had happened, the plane couldn't be accessed by the gate crew. But a Southwest employee stepped into the breach, searching the empty plane and returning the laptop, which had rolled from Suckow's seat all the way to the back of the plane.

Suckow not only wrote about the encounter in an industry publication, she came back to the airport to personally hand Southwest employee Chad Johnson a thank-you note and a copy of the magazine article in which the incident was featured. The gate agent called Johnson up from the tarmac and handed the PA mike to Suckow, who excitedly told her story. Everyone within earshot in the terminal erupted into applause, every Southwest employee in sight beamed proudly, and poor Chad Johnson—caught unaware—looked shocked and a bit overwhelmed.

This story is unusual not just because we hear so few tales of exceptional customer service in the airline industry, but also because the employee involved was not in a customer-facing role. He was neither a gate agent nor a flight attendant. His job was to service the aircraft once passengers had deplaned.

Johnson turned down Suckow's offer of a tip when he returned the laptop, saying he was just "doing his job." And to him, the job entailed going the extra distance to take care of a passenger he'd never met, in order to correct a problem that was certainly not the airline's fault. The outcome was a powerful boost to the Southwest brand, not just for Shawna Suckow, but for the hundreds of passengers like me who witnessed this event unfold.

If you think this story could happen on any airline, let me tell you it is not likely to be United. A senior United Airlines flight attendant recently told me United personnel are strongly discouraged from doing *anything* that deviates from the company's standard operating practice—whether it's adding humor to those boring safety messages, as Southwest flight attendants often do, changing any part of their uniform (even in relation to a holiday or special event), or sharing destination information with a passenger on an iPad. Seems to me United has missed the flight on this one.

Many organizations invest hundreds of thousands or even millions of dollars in branding campaigns. If they've done their homework, they'll train sales reps and customer service personnel on the key messages that will be promoted in these campaigns. But very few actually take the time to educate the entire organization from top to bottom on what these messages are, how they integrate with the values of the company, and how they impact each individual—whatever his role—in the way he does his job.

Sometimes the individual with the most impact might be the doorman who smiles and offers helpful advice rather than standing stone-faced, his attention elsewhere as he robotically opens the door. Other times, it's the cable repairperson who arrives on time, solves a problem the homeowner didn't know he had, and suggests additional ways to get the most from the cable system—rather than grudgingly fixing an issue after an extended wait and offering no more than a few unintelligible grunts. In either case, these employees can be your best marketers—or your worst nightmares.

Customer-Facing Employees Can Make or Break You

Unhappy employees have always led to unhappy customers, but today the repercussions are much broader because every interaction has the potential to be broadcast nearly instantly to a global audience. In an age when information is shared freely and quickly on a worldwide basis, there's nowhere to hide. The way a company treats its employees is mirrored in the way those employees then treat customers, and in the way customers view the company. That's why the actions, attitudes, and behaviors of your customer-facing employees can make or break you.

Creating a good impression in customers' minds goes beyond making sure employees are neat, well dressed, polite, and helpful. It means that everyone from the delivery person to the doorman should be actively engaged in representing your brand—in the way you want to be represented.

Employees Are the Clear Choice for Great Ideas

The team at Caribou Coffee thinks it's critical to develop a differentiated brand personality. So much so that the company doesn't take itself too seriously. Caribou Coffee has developed a brand personality that is fun and playful. According to Michele Vig, vice president of marketing, because Caribou Coffee is small, it can take more risks.

Take, for example, the 2014 launch of Caribou's Clear Coffee. Haven't heard of it? Well, consider that it launched on April 1. And it was gone by April 2. Vig says Caribou Coffee had been looking for a fun idea for April Fool's Day. The company's agency partner generated ideas, but the pranks were expensive and elaborate. Vig decided to send an e-mail to the entire company offering $200 for the winning idea. Twenty-four hours later, she had received hundreds of ideas. Not only did Caribou Coffee have a fun April Fool's Day promotion, but the marketing team unearthed lot of other good ideas as well. Vig put the ideas generated into four buckets: (1) those that weren't really that good, (2) those that would be great for April Fool's Day, (3) those that really should be considered *beyond* April Fool's Day, and (4) "Uh-oh. If we did that, we'd probably get arrested."

Vig is focusing more on open idea generation. She notes brand is culture and culture is brand. People want to participate. "When marketing acts like they know everything, no one wants to partner with us," she says.

Which Comes First: Customers or Employees?

Several years ago, when I taught a graduate-level marketing class on internal branding, I asked my students which was more important, customers or employees. Students made persuasive arguments on one side or the other. Without customers, there's no reason to have employees. Yet, without employees, how will we get any customers?

This is one of those chicken-and-egg discussions. The right answer, in my book, is that customers and employees are equally important. Focusing on one to the exclusion of the other may work for a short time, but in the long term it's a recipe for disaster. Successful businesses need both groups to be engaged and empowered when it comes to promoting an organization's brand and driving key marketing initiatives.

In reality, employees are often the last to be considered when it comes to communication about branding and marketing campaigns. It's almost as if they are included as an afterthought. We know we need to reach customers with a set of key messages, but employees? Too often they get the hand-me-downs, if anything at all.

Yet employees are *the* voice and face of your business to the customer. That means *all* customer-facing employees need to be exposed to and internalize key elements of the corporate brand. And, in one way or another, *all* employees are eventually customers. When they truly understand what the brand stands for, employees will rise to the challenge and represent the organization appropriately.

Anyone who walks into an Apple Store knows the employees there truly embody the spirit and values of the Apple brand. From the assigned greeter who smiles at you as you enter the door to the cheerful, eager, and knowledgeable people who staff the Genius Bar, every employee understands the essence of the Apple brand. Just as importantly, they are empowered to use their talents and best judgment to help others. Interestingly, these employees are not on commission. In fact, they don't seem to care whether the customer makes an incremental purchase. They've happily helped me with Apple products not purchased directly through Apple, and we've gotten the same cheerful, helpful service in Sydney, Australia, that we did in Palo Alto, California.

This kind of employee-customer engagement doesn't happen overnight. It doesn't happen because an executive issues a decree to "Be cheerful, eager, and helpful—or else!" It happens because Apple hires helpful, passionate people to work at its stores. But even more importantly, it happens because Apple understands that the tone and demeanor of the interactions customers have with Apple Store employees convey key messages about the Apple brand.

On the purchase process scale outlined in chapter 3, Apple is far to the right, focused on driving loyalty and evangelism. One of the key ways the company has achieved its exemplary level of loyalty is by taking employee engagement seriously.

Guiding the Way for Employees

You don't have to be Apple to get employee engagement right, as shown by the example of Atlanta-based CredAbility. Credit counseling began in the United States in the early 1960s as a face-to-face community service. The advent of national 800-number phone service and then the Internet expanded access and service options, and for the first time credit counseling was able to break the barriers of time, location, and channel.

Consumer Credit Counseling Service of Greater Atlanta was one among more than a hundred organizations that existed under the moniker "CCCS."

One of the few organizations that seized this opportunity to invest in the technology and infrastructure to deliver ubiquitous service to its clients, CCCS of Greater Atlanta grew to become the third largest national provider of credit counseling services in the United States.

However, with more than a hundred organizations still using the CCCS moniker, there was significant confusion. A series of mergers meant CCCS of Greater Atlanta had offices in five states. The "...of Greater Atlanta" description characterized the organization as a regional service provider, when, in fact, it served clients in all fifty states and three territories, 24–7, in English and Spanish.

According to Mike Siegel, former senior vice president of marketing and chief communications officer, adopting a national identity as CredAbility provided a platform that allowed the organization to differentiate and distinguish itself from other credit counseling groups. "It also helped us communicate our national service footprint as we appealed for increasingly limited philanthropic contributions," he said.

Siegel knew he had to empower employees to represent the new brand. In this case, the counselors who worked with consumers were the face of the company. To help them, Siegel's team created a hard copy guide to the new brand, outlining what it stood for and how employees would engage with the CredAbility brand. The guide included everything from frequently asked questions (FAQs) about the name change to templates for answering the phone correctly and creating appropriate e-mail signatures.

Siegel says that in one sense, it felt like the guide was overkill. Yet it turned out the tool was exactly what employees needed. "People want to do the right thing. If you give them the tools and relevant information and make it important, they'll do this. Otherwise, they make it up and that may not be what you need," he said.

The proof this approach was successful? Several years later the organization merged with another nonprofit and rebranded again. The first question from employees was, "Where's our brand guidebook?"

Inside-Out Marketing: the Importance of Internal Engagement

Liz Kelly, CEO of Brilliant Ink, a San Francisco Bay Area employee engagement consulting firm, has thoroughly studied the mechanics of employee engagement. Her research has shown that employee experience correlates strongly with employee engagement. Kelly has looked specifically at employees' key moments on the job, from the day they start at a company until the day they leave. Her goal was to understand what influences employee engagement and to identify those factors that organizations can control from a programmatic standpoint.

Kelly says, "We had a hunch that if you did these things well, you would see a difference in terms of overall employee engagement. But we didn't know that we would see that correlation in pretty much every area looked at—and it's all statistically significant." According to Kelly, a fantastic orientation experience stays with employees for up to seven years (perhaps even longer—Kelly's research only looked at seven years of employee experience). People remember their orientation and onboarding experiences, and what they remember about these experiences correlates with how deeply they engage with the organization on an ongoing basis.

FIGURE 10-1: Employees Project the Message

The challenge is that there's no single accepted definition of employee engagement. Nor are there universally accepted metrics for measuring

the effectiveness of employee engagement initiatives. What works in one organization may not fit another, which means you'll need to create a program that suits your company's needs.

Have you thought about the ways you can engage employees at your organization? Don't delegate this task to Human Resources. Including multiple parts of the organization is an important way that smart companies can differentiate themselves and get above the noise.

Dirty Laundry Will Always Come Out

Remember those old family secrets you weren't supposed to talk about? It was easy to sweep those skeletons under the bed. But that's not the case when it comes to organizations. No one is perfect. We all have history we'd prefer not be aired publicly. However, when the secret relates to an organization's internal employee disputes—whether over wages, working conditions, or a general disdain for management—presume that the information will come out one way or another. And it's not likely these types of disclosures will reflect favorably on your organization or on your brand.

If you can, defuse potential issues before they escalate. When that's not possible and you're faced with a crisis, be honest and forthright. Admit what you know and what you don't. Commit to communicating regularly, consistently, and with a high degree of integrity.

A better way to avoid crisis situations is by engaging employees proactively. Liz Kelly says you need to help employees feel empowered by connecting the dots between the employee's work and the bigger picture of the organization's goals. The more employees feel connected to the organization's goals, the more likely it is that they'll be highly engaged.

Marketing plays an important role here. If messages to employees are too dry, they'll be ignored. But if employees feel like they're being sold to, they'll tune out. It's all about balance. You'll need to come up with a strategy that enlists frontline employees in not only living the brand but in creating ongoing customer engagement as well.

Setting the Table

Niki Leondakis is the CEO of Commune Hotels & Resorts, a hospitality company formed by the merger of two smaller regional hotel companies, one based in San Francisco and one in New York. Leondakis was formerly the president of Kimpton Hotels, a hospitality chain that is number one in its segment in customer service and has been named as one of the Fortune Top 100 best places to work for four years running.

Leondakis decided that the key way to get employees engaged and representing the Commune brand identity was to develop a higher purpose—similar to the noble sales purpose Lisa McLeod discussed in chapter 8. To do this, she enlisted the entire organization. Leondakis conducted company-wide meetings, gathered feedback and input, and asked employees to participate in a conversation about what they wanted the Commune brand to represent.

Over an eight-month period, the initial list of seventy-seven core values was narrowed down to ten core values that make up the "Spirit of Commune." From this, the organization developed a single key statement of higher purpose: *Commune Hotels is dedicated to creating transformational experiences that inspire the human spirit.*

This focus is not just for paying customers, but for all the people who engage with Commune. That includes employees, real estate partners, business owners, vendors, and the communities in which the firm does business. It infuses not just the way Commune treats guests, but also the way the hotels engage with vendors. It means the company ensures it can live up to the commitments it makes. It informs the way Commune conducts business meetings and corporate reviews. Leondakis asks, "How can we do a P&L review in a way that's inspiring and transformative to our business partners?"

That statement of purpose also ties into the core of Commune's marketing and communications efforts. The company's marketing team uses the purpose statement as the core of the company's branding. Joie de Vivre, Commune's California brand, is lighthearted and casual, so transformative experiences there may be more fun, quirky,

and playful. Another of Commune's brands, Thompson Hotels, is more sophisticated—stylish and urban. In 2015, the company is introducing a third brand, Tommie, that will combine elements of its existing two brands. Creating a transformative experience needs to tie directly into the mission of each brand—from the imagery on the Website to the tone of the marketing campaigns.

From an internal perspective, the new Commune purpose was rolled out through a series of focused employee communications programs. It started with a worldwide "listening tour" by Leondakis that included fireside chats with frontline employees. It continued with "Notes from Niki," weekly e-mail blasts to all company employees that focused on Leondakis's observations about visits to various properties. In these weekly communications, Leondakis often recognized individuals who were embodying the spirit of transformation, as she reinforced key elements of the new culture.

After sixteen months, the "Notes from Niki" have evolved into videos that are hosted on an online portal, which also features stories, guest letters, and e-mails from one employee to another. Transparency is key. Leondakis also does regular Twitter chats where anyone can jump in— guests, customers, even competitors.

How is this working? Commune has put measurement systems in place. On the customer side, the company reviews such metrics as customer service scores, social media rankings, and TripAdvisor reviews. Internally, the goal is to make sure that the ten core values that make up the "Spirit of Commune" are coming across in every interaction— whether it's an e-mail conversation or a phone call, a meeting or a presentation to a partner.

Leondakis says a good rollout is not enough: "We have to be intensely committed to reaffirming this, celebrating success, and talking about our belief system, our higher purpose, our values every single day. We want to instill pride in the troops that this is who we are. We're not just corporate America. We stand for more. And we're a part of something that's good in this world."

Fixing the Sour Notes at the Ritz-Carlton

Several years ago, I attended a consulting workshop at the Ritz-Carlton Resort in Naples, Florida. I had just come from the ten-day Sonata piano camp for adults in Bennington, Vermont. Upon my return to San Francisco, I was scheduled to play a recital as a benefit for my teacher's music school.

I'm a fairly accomplished amateur pianist. Having come from an intense week of practice, I knew my music was well-polished and ready for an audience. I also knew the importance the Ritz-Carlton places on keeping guests satisfied. The Ritz goes the extra distance to take care of guests' needs. Late one afternoon when there weren't many people around, I asked one of the servers if I there was a piano I could use. He directed me to a nice Steinway piano a short distance away. I sat down and proceeded to launch into a Bach toccata.

About ten minutes later, a rather nervous-looking man in a drab suit came by and stood at the piano, glaring at me. "I'm with Loss Prevention!" he informed me. "And you can't play that piano!" I looked at him in disbelief. "Well, actually, I can," I said. "And quite well."

"There must be some misunderstanding," I told him. "A Ritz employee directed me to this piano. And why am I speaking with Loss Prevention? Are you really afraid I'm going to try to steal the piano? Perhaps I might take a few of the keys with me?"

"No, of course not," he said. "But you are *not* allowed to play the piano!" And off he stormed. A few minutes later, he was back, accompanied by another nervous man who introduced himself as a hotel manager. "It's against the Ritz-Carlton policy for guests to play our pianos," he proclaimed. "Whoever told you otherwise was mistaken."

"Is there a problem with my playing?" I asked.

"No," he said. "I've studied music myself and you're actually quite good. But we have a policy and I have to enforce it."

Talk about striking the wrong chord. This was so diametrically opposed to everything I had heard and knew about the way the Ritz treated its customers. The next morning I spoke with the senior manager

at the hotel. I told him I knew that Ritz employees had the discretion to spend up to $2,500 without prior approval to satisfy unhappy guests. I told him how well taken care of I'd been since I'd arrived at the hotel and how attentive just about all of their employees had been. He smiled broadly. I told him I taught a graduate level course on internal branding, and that we used the Ritz-Carlton as an exemplar of a company that really taught employees well in this regard. Now he was beaming. "Which is why," I said, "I am so disappointed that I'll have to stop using the Ritz-Carlton as my example." He stopped smiling immediately.

I related the details of the previous day's incident. He listened quietly, swallowed hard, and said, "Thank you. The only way we at the Ritz can maintain our high level of quality is to find out about these types of incidents where we don't measure up to our own standards. I'm going to go speak to Loss Prevention to discuss how poorly this has been handled," he said. "Then we'll use this as a case study at the next employee meeting, so that our entire team can learn from the incident."

The piano policy was created to stop small children from banging on the pianos, which is extremely disruptive to the ambience of the hotel. However, that was certainly not the case here. Ritz employees should have applied discretion (as the first employee did), to allow for a different situation.

Did this mean there would be a piano I could play on the following day? "Absolutely," he said.

Not only did the Ritz-Carlton solve the problem, the company used it to set an example of the way the ladies and gentlemen of the Ritz are expected to treat the ladies and gentlemen they serve. Stories like this become part of the culture. They ensure that *all* customer-facing people (even Loss Prevention!) understand the important role they play in influencing customers.

11

Can Social Sharing Amplify Your Reach?

If you listen to many marketers, you'd think that marketing in the twenty-first century is driven totally by social media. In June 2014, Gallup released a report that noted only 5 percent of more than eighteen thousand U.S. consumers polled said social media had a great deal of influence on their buying decisions. In fact, 62 percent of those surveyed said social media had *no* influence at all on what they chose to buy.[1]

Gallup found this to be true across all age groups—including millennials, "a generation that many companies regard as a key social media audience." According to Gallup, more than 94 percent of those who use social media do so to connect with friends and families. Only 29 percent use social media to find product reviews and information.[2] This explains why many companies find social media are not providing the marketing lift above the noise they expected.

In 2013, an ad campaign helped Ritz-Carlton Hotels increase the number of its Facebook fans dramatically. The problem was that the hotel chain wasn't able to effectively engage with its newly enlarged community, now nearly half a million strong. Rather than focusing on expansion of its fan base, today Ritz-Carlton directs attention to engaging existing fans and analyzing social media conversations.[3]

While companies may reach hundreds of thousands of fans on Facebook or followers on Twitter, not all of these fans and followers have equal weight. Some are associated with fake or automated accounts. Others are people who are not necessarily part of the brand's target audience.[4]

The question then becomes, where and when should marketers use social channels to help raise marketing efforts above the noise? Let's look at how to choose the right social tools for your situation. We'll also address how to understand the real costs your organization incurs when implementing social programs.

With Friends Like These, Who Needs Enemies?

It's important to remember that social media are tactics and tools. These come and go on a regular basis. I'd bet good money that a new social media platform will be created between the time I write these words and the time you read them. The question is which, if any, of these social media tools are right for your organization.

As the folks from the Ritz-Carlton learned, success in the social media arena is not about quantity, but *quality*. Having millions of followers means nothing if they are not the people you want to reach, or if you have to buy their "fandom." And it's not a good use of scarce time and money if you don't *do* something to reach out to the people who have chosen to identify with your organization.

While it's important to integrate the best set of tools possible, remember your goal is to grow your business, not to keep up with the latest fads and trends. That means using the correct tools to meet your needs and keeping track of the entire marketing picture.

One can certainly create a strategy that includes social media implementation. However, "use social media" is not in itself a sound marketing strategy. Instead, focus on making sure you have the right vehicle to reach the right audience. Your target audience is likely the people who can purchase or influence the purchase of your product or service. It might also be employees, vendors, and suppliers, or even the local community.

Whichever audience you choose, you'll need to go where they go and reach them in the way they want to be reached. Don't use the Golden Rule (treat others the way *you* would like to be treated). Try instead the Platinum Rule (treat others as *they* would like to be treated).

Consider this. Your marketing strategy is the road, and the tactics you use to reach them are the vehicles. Although a sleek Ferrari might be fun to drive on clear, fast roads, a four-wheel drive SUV makes more sense when you're navigating snow on your way to the ski slopes. And there are places where an old-fashioned bicycle, or even your own two feet, is the best mode of transportation.

Social media have developed an excellent set of listening tools. The key focus on *listening* means that you have to stop *talking* long enough to hear what's being said. Ask your marketing team:

- Do you know to whom you should be listening?
- Do you know where you're likely to find them?
- Do you have a good way to monitor the social chatter in those channels?

Everybody's a Reporter . . . and a Critic

With the advent of citizen journalism, everyone with a camera is a reporter. Everyone with a keyboard is a columnist. Everyone with a mobile device can express his sentiments on world events or on your business or products. As a result, the way the public defines media—and the way media define themselves—has changed. News travels at near real-time speeds, and so do rumors, fads, and scares.

Individuals now define themselves not just in terms of the number of friends or followers they have, but also by the communities they belong to and the content they create. They listen in on the conversations of those they barely know. They also know more about the status of casual acquaintances than one ever thought possible. Everyone wants to jump on the bandwagon. The question is, what does it mean? Ask:

- Are the people who like you the ones who matter to you?
- Are the people who follow you likely to become your customers?

- Are those people who connect to you likely to either purchase or influence the purchase of your product or service?
- If the answer to any of the above three questions is no, how can you connect with the right people in the future?

Context Counts

As of early 2014, Facebook had more than 1.3 billion subscribers.[5] At a 23 percent annual growth rate, by the time you read this, the subscriber number will likely be somewhere north of 1.6 billion. It also means it's likely most of your customers and potential customers will be on Facebook at one time or another. Does that mean Facebook is the ideal vehicle for marketing your product or service? Not necessarily.

The problem is context. While most of your target audience may indeed have a Facebook account, many of them are using it for specific purposes. They are likely connecting with old friends, recounting weekend or vacation exploits, and posting pictures of friends, family, and pets (and those ubiquitous cat videos!).

If you have a consumer-focused product, like Wrigley's Skittles, Facebook may be the perfect place to be. But what if your offering is targeted at a B2B audience or a subgroup of people who use Facebook in a limited fashion? Or what if it is not a product people regularly associate with Facebook? In that case, putting your focus on a Facebook marketing campaign may be a total waste of time. Worse yet, you may alienate the very people you want to reach by hitting them with messages they consider spam.

It's important to understand the context in which your customers connect with a social media platform. It's also critical to use a platform for its strengths. As Eric Schmidt, chairman and former CEO of Google, noted, "If content is king, context is its crown."[6]

Twitter, for example, is both a great listening mechanism and a way to respond quickly to fast-breaking events. It is not, however, the best tool for general promotion. Why? Because Twitter users are looking for useful information, not marketing hype. They will tune out or stop following you if they think you are not providing them with valuable content.

YouTube is great for short videos (under three minutes) or for longer technical "how-to" training sessions. It is likely not as useful for lengthy monologues or extended shots of talking heads holding forth on your product or company. By the time you've hit three minutes, you'll likely have lost a lot of your audience.

The Medium Is No Longer the Message

For decades, communications professionals have been quoting Marshall McLuhan, the Canadian communication theorist who said that the medium is the message. To McLuhan, it was the communication medium, not the content the medium carries, that was critical. He also said that the characteristics of the medium itself affected society as much as the content conveyed over that medium.[7]

That may have been true once upon a time, but it's not necessarily true today. Today we are drowning in media options. In our current environment, people don't choose only one medium through which to receive information. Consumers latch on to content from a variety of sources, online and off. I'd argue that today the *content i*s the message, regardless of the medium in which it is delivered. And today that content is likely to be delivered in multiple media simultaneously.

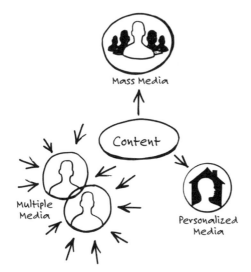

FIGURE 11-1: Content Is the Message

Whereas in the past we had mass media (one medium reaching masses of people), today we have multiple media (multiple media reaching out to each of us individually) and personalized media (delivery mechanisms customized to individual preferences). The differences are profound.

We've talked about how interactive marketers look at media as paid, owned, earned, and shared. But what they're really focusing on is the *content* that is shared. Of course, you still need to customize a message to the medium. A tweet can be no longer than 140 characters; YouTube video requires, well, video, not characters; and a Vine video can be no longer than six seconds. But to rise above the noise, the message we are trying to convey and the conversations in which we are trying to engage must be consistent from one medium to the next. This is true even though the choice of media may differ by individual. The discussion needs to go beyond the medium used to deliver it.

Media will change in the future. In five years, we'll likely be able to choose media options that don't exist today. The question is, how will marketers be able to transcend those choices to get their message heard above the noise?

Using Social Sharing to Save Lives

Imagine that your organization offers a technology that could potentially save the lives of hundreds of thousands or even millions of soon-to-be-born children. Imagine also that this technology is still a promise. It may be decades in the future before this promise is realized, if ever. However, the chance to participate is either realized or rejected in the few moments after each child's birth.

That's the situation facing Cord Blood Registry (CBR). The company offers parents the ability to bank the stem cells found in their newborn child's umbilical cord. The goal is to have those cells available in the future to treat diseases that may be cured through regenerative medicine (stem cell therapy). CBR has already banked more than half a million sets of cord blood and cord tissue stem cells.

The challenge the company faces is cutting through all of the noise surrounding expectant parents to make them aware of the possibility of cord blood banking. They want these parents to let their OB/GYNs know they'd like to participate in the program, well before they go into labor. Yet the conversation between doctor and patient about cord blood banking today is usually less than five minutes long.

Vice president of marketing Tia Newcomer arrived at CBR in April 2013. Previously, the scientific and medical affairs group led marketing at the company, which resulted in a very scientific approach to content. In addition, CBR's former CEO had equated marketing with PR, which led to a very narrow focus. Newcomer's prior experience included stints at such companies as Hewlett-Packard and PepsiCo. She knew that, to get above the noise, she had to change the CBR brand and the way the company approached marketing.

There are, on average, four million live births per year in the United States. About half of those families are in a position to purchase CBR services. Yet today only 5 percent of these bank their newborn's cord blood. To get above the noise, CBR needs to focus on education. The first area of focus is customers. "I was given a lot of market data—which is great to have, but it's not customer data," Newcomer says. "I wanted to hear what customers think about the brand, what they think about the category—what I call the path to purchase."

Second, Newcomer realized she had no one with digital marketing competency on her team. "Everybody in marketing, every person on your team, has to have digital acumen—an understanding and passion for digital. I'd argue that the entire marketing organization could be called a digital marketing organization," she said. "I had no one on my team who had any of that experience."

Newcomer has focused CBR on developing good content. Facebook is a critical community for the company. When she first came on board, CBR had about forty-five thousand followers, and its Facebook posts were very scientific in focus. Now CBR's Facebook page has undergone a "face lift" based on the company's new branding, plus there's a renewed focus on posting daily with engaging content. "Our team comes up with really great parenting plus science," she says. "They have really consumerized the content, so it's engaging content that's being shared."

A year later, CBR's Facebook page had close to 150,000 followers.

Posts typically get more than sixty comments. Some posts have hundreds or even thousands of likes and shares. CBR is also personalizing the content it offers. In the old world, no matter how people came to the company or what they asked, they received the same prepackaged content in return. Today, Newcomer's team has more than twenty different content tracks to respond to customer requests, and that number continues to grow. "We've got to have engagement that's personalized and customized, and that starts with engaging content," she says.

The third area of focus is community. "We had very little community. There were thousands of communities that should be talking about your product and your brand," said Newcomer. "We had no place to feed them information and give them things to share. And we had no place to really pull them all together and make them passionate about what we knew the power of our product was—which was not only curing known disease today, but treating a whole list of diseases that have no known cure yet."

Today, half of CBR's business comes from repeat customers (parents having additional children) and from referrals. The other half is new business. New business is extremely important to CBR, because these customers will refer their friends and become repeat customers if they have more children.

How has the new focus on marketing impacted CBR? In Newcomer's first year at the company, CBR's new business has grown more than 5 percent. This came by listening to customers, engaging with them differently, and giving them the content they want. And it's the first new business growth the company has seen in nearly eight years.

CBR's audience is changing too, as more and more millennials approach childbearing age. "There's definitely an importance placed on that altruistic common good for the whole of humanity," she says. "We have partnerships with public cord banks. We encourage parents to donate their stem cells. It's not public versus private, or private industry fighting among a small piece of business. This is really about educating people about their choices, so that they either save cord blood or donate it. That's really what we want. It's the trash can that's the enemy here," she adds.

No Such Thing as a Free Lunch

People consider social media to be free—probably because there's no out-of-pocket media cost, like there is with paid advertising or promotion. But with social media, as with everything else, there is no such thing as a free lunch. While anyone can play in the social media sphere without paying an access fee, the costs can be enormous.

FIGURE 11-2: The Three Types of Marketing Investment

There's the cost of assigning a resource to manage social media projects. Setting up a Twitter feed or a Facebook account or a YouTube channel is nice, but unless you are monitoring these channels in real time and keeping the content fresh, nothing good will happen for you. In fact, bad things can happen. Your customers may be leaving comments that you don't see and therefore you can't provide a timely response.

Posting on social media without the correct content is not only a waste of time and money, it can hurt you badly as well. Content needs to be thoughtfully curated for each audience and channel. Furthermore, it's helpful to have company guidelines that make it clear who can post on behalf of the organization, the types of comments they should be posting, and, more importantly, the things they should *not* be saying or doing on behalf of the organization.

Remember that there's always a trade-off for the time and effort required to support social tools. The time spent in managing a low-traffic Facebook page is time that can't be put into a potentially more effective marketing program. Whatever medium you choose will require ongoing feeding and attention—with the right people involved.

There's another area of investment, too: expertise. If you aren't using people with the right skills and expertise to deliver a marketing program, you'll likely wind up spending much more time and money when all is said and done.

Marketer Mike Siegel reminisces that there was a time when *everyone* had to do a newsletter, whether it was the best tactic or not. "Newsletters often turned into black holes that sucked up resources you never got back," says Siegel. Once you started, you wound up continuing to feed the beast. To a certain extent, that's what's happening with social media today, notes Siegel. Social media are iterative, real-time marketing tactics that can be extremely time consuming if done well. They set expectations for responsiveness, care and feeding, and differentiation. How much of a professional communications person's time each week does it take to support these initiatives? Are these campaigns worth it?

At CredAbility, Siegel looked at Nielsen BuzzMetrics. Siegel's team knew there were conversations taking place in the cloud that were topical and relevant to the organization, but they weren't necessarily in the places one might think. That's because conversations about credit counseling and financial crisis are very personal and can be quite emotional, even embarrassing. These are not the types of conversations that consumers tend to "like" on Facebook. So rather than driving for more likes, CredAbility started engaging in conversations about how to seek financial help, answering common questions, and polling on relevant topics.

For CredAbility, Twitter became a way to stimulate news media interest on topics and trends and to generate strong media relationships. The organization's Twitter account was managed by its PR team, while its Facebook presence was managed by the marketing team.

Tomorrow Is Always a Day Away

There'll always be something new over the horizon if we just wait for tomorrow. When it comes to social sharing platforms, we know there will be new techniques evolving on a regular basis. While you don't want to jump on every bandwagon that roars into town, you don't want to sit on the sidelines forever either.

Some of these new platforms will be good, some will be bad. Some will dramatically improve our effectiveness. Others will be ineffective. What's common to all is that they are all untested and unproven. So how do we move forward? Here are a few guidelines:

- **Jump in and test.** See what works for your organization. Do this on a small scale so that you are able to pull the plug if you don't see results. But know in advance what constitutes "good" results.
- **Watch and wait.** See what others are doing. Learn from their mistakes. If it looks like there's value, consider jumping in yourself.
- **Go where the people are.** In ancient times, markets grew up where people were gathering. Follow that logic today. Go where your customers and prospects gather. Watch and listen and see what catches their attention. Use new tools on a case-by-case basis, just as you would use chopsticks in a Chinese restaurant but not for a hamburger and fries.
- **Look for crossover.** Often, a new way of communicating will be added to an existing tool. LinkedIn is very different today than it was a few years ago. It has features that are very Facebook- and Twitter-like. Yet it exists for a totally different audience and purpose. Look for creative ways to use existing platforms, without reinventing the wheel.

When Your Audience Isn't Very Social

What happens when your audience isn't overly inspired by social media? At BMC Software, former head of marketing Kim DeCarlis knew her

B2B audience was unlikely to connect with the company on Facebook. They were much more likely to pay attention to Twitter and LinkedIn. "You have to understand that your customers aren't necessarily coming to you. You need to go to them," she says. "Where are they congregating to learn about products like yours? Are they going to a computing Website? Do they follow a blogger? Do they go to your Website?"

Combining paid, earned, shared, and owned media can be powerful, DeCarlis notes. "You have to pay to play in some places. You have to provide good content and earn placement on channels for thought leadership and media. With social, you have to inspire people to share. And, ultimately, you are a publisher. You have to make sure that people come to channels that you own because at the end of the day, it's all about the content."

Content creation isn't always the responsibility of the marketing team. At BMC, for example, the responsibility was shared among marketing, the product groups, the office of the CTO, and other areas of the company.

DeCarlis notes that content needs to be both created and curated. It's particularly important to affiliate with thought leaders who have interesting points of view. As such, BMC worked to build alliances with thought leaders in the cloud and developer operations space.

The More Things Change...

How social should your organization be to stand out above the noise? As social as it needs to be, but not more than necessary.

Go back to the basics, the fundamentals: know your customers, your market, and your product. Then find the best way to communicate the value you provide. Sometimes that will be through public social media channels. Sometimes it will be by creating your own community. In other cases, it means creating outstanding content for your audiences to digest across their existing communities.

Creating interest about your offering is important. Stoking the fires of conversation to keep your offering top of mind is a requisite for success. Understanding your customers is critical.

The techniques you use are less relevant than the fact that you are there to listen and to understand what's important. Remember, social tools are techniques to help amplify your reach. You still need to be creating an impactful message targeted to the relevant audience. Otherwise, you may find yourself amplifying the wrong things.

PART IV

Above the Noise

12

Momentum Factors for Success

I'm a pretty good intermediate skier... I can get down just about any slope, but it won't always be pretty. I'll work my way slowly and deliberately, with a great deal of effort, down a tough trail. Several years ago I hired a ski instructor to help me learn how to ski moguls, those "bumps" on the trail that the pros navigate so effortlessly, but which I'd never been able to master. The instructor watched me ski slowly and painfully down the trail before making a comment that resounded with me as a musician. "Every mountain has its own speed or tempo. If you ski too fast, you'll wipe out. But if you ski too slow, you won't get enough speed to be able to connect the turns and create momentum."

I knew this was true in music. We've all heard new musicians play a piece so slowly that all we can hear are the individual notes, not the music. I've come to realize this is true for business as well. Sometimes we need to put our personal style aside and understand the situation itself. We need to let the environment set the pace. Just like a golfer adapts to each new golf course or a mountain climber uses the face of the rock to rappel down the mountain, we need to leverage our environment to create momentum for success.

The Five Momentum Factors

Over my career as a marketing professional, I've seen marketing from the agency side, the corporate perspective, and now from the consultant's viewpoint. What I've realized is that while understanding the Dynamic Market Leverage Factors—the eight timeless marketing truths— outlined in this book is critical to building a successful marketing organization, it's not sufficient. There are far too many organizations that focused on what appears to be "the right stuff," yet still didn't deliver as promised or weren't considered successful.

I've had the opportunity to work at the intersection of marketing and organization development in my consulting work. This led me to identify other factors that might have a key role in marketing success, factors that relate to the business environment itself. These factors are likely to be important for other parts of the company as well, but they're certainly key for the marketing organization.

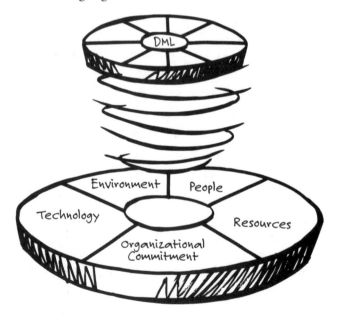

FIGURE 12-1: Momentum Factors

To return to the skiing example, these five momentum leverage factors provide the extra oomph—the momentum—it takes to get down the hill with power and finesse rather than winding up in a crumpled mess at the bottom of the slope.

These factors help you navigate the internal environment of your organization and your marketplace. It's not enough to understand marketing by itself, you need to understand how to apply these concepts given the internal workings of your organization. It's not enough to work *at* marketing. It's just as important to know how to work *within* the organization.

1. Organizational Commitment

The best marketing organization in the world will not be successful without the support of the larger business or organization of which it is a part. Time and time again, we see creative and innovative marketing teams tilting at windmills in an attempt to get acceptance and buy-in for their endeavors. In many of these organizations, marketing is seen as an expense, or perhaps a necessary evil—something that likely must be funded, but only grudgingly.

In fairness to the folks making these decisions, they often see the marketing team as creating frenetic energy that adds to all the noise in the system. In many marketing organizations, there's lots of activity, but no way to track or measure success, and no strategic plan. They don't know what marketing intends to accomplish or how to determine if these results were actually achieved.

However, even with a strategic marketing plan, success requires solid organizational support. This starts at the top. Your chief executive and her direct reports need to understand the value of effective marketing. Otherwise, they're not likely to provide the support necessary for marketing success. Too many executives treat marketing as the execution team—the ones who are there to create the pretty banners, the fun giveaways, and the cool-looking Website. This attitude quickly carries from the top down through the rest of the organization.

When things get tough, if executives don't see the value of marketing, it will be the first area to be cut. Those who *do* understand the potential return will be more likely to continue making marketing investments on an ongoing basis. It's up to you, as a marketing leader, to ensure that people understand the importance of marketing to the overall business.

Talent expert Roberta Matuson, president of Matuson Consulting and author of *Talent Magnetism* and *Suddenly in Charge,* says that if you're a leader who doesn't manage up, you won't have to worry about managing down for very long. You'll be taken out by a tidal wave you never saw coming. The good news: managing up is a skill you can learn. Matuson says senior leaders really *want* to be managed. In fact, they often prefer that you tell them what you're going to do rather than asking them what you should do next.

We don't expect to plant seeds in the morning and harvest vegetables that evening. It takes proper nurturing, care, and nutrients—as well as time—to grow beautiful tomatoes or pick tasty fruit from a tree. Marketing initiatives are the same way. Plant in the spring for a bountiful harvest later in the year. Or perhaps plant this year for buckets of fruit in the years to come.

One way to know you've developed a respected marketing organization is when the marketing group is included in strategic business discussions. This means the CMO or top marketing executive must work collaboratively with other key functions. But it also means that executive management must support and enable this collaboration. Too often, individual functions are compensated on independent performance and goals, which encourages a silo-type mentality.

How do you manage your managers and peers more effectively? Take the time to work inside the organization. Educate your colleagues and peers about what you're doing and why. Teaching them about audience and messages is an easy conversation. The harder task is to convey the full import of marketing—but that's the conversation that counts.

Build relationships. Engage the organization in what's happening but be sure not to lecture colleagues in other departments. Elicit their feedback. It's less about posturing with a dog-and-pony show and more about letting people live the value with you, as the Commune Hotel group does with its statement of higher purpose. If you do this well, you will build champions who not only understand marketing's importance to the organization, but who then become your evangelists.

2. Resources

It's not enough to have good intentions. You also need to have the resources to create and manage successful marketing initiatives. Too many good marketing organizations have failed because not enough resources were allocated to develop and execute outstanding marketing campaigns.

On the road to marketing success, consider strategy the road map and execution the vehicle. Financial resources are the fuel. What good does it do to plan an exciting expedition and get everyone in the car, only to be left by the side of the road because you've run out of gas? I've very rarely found a marketing executive who told me that she had more than enough resources to accomplish her goals. This is as true of large organizations as it is of start-ups. As the company scales, so do the demands placed on marketing.

However, it's one thing to have enough money to fund only the key components of marketing—to resource at least the critical pieces of the eight Dynamic Market Leverage Factors discussed earlier. It's another to be underfunded to the point that you can't even keep the lights on, so to speak. What senior executives don't always realize is that there's a minimum threshold at which resources allocated to marketing can make a difference. It's one thing to have a budget and another to have enough of a budget to make things happen.

Below a certain threshold, dollars are simply wasted. It's been proven that most consumers need to see a message seven times within a reasonable time frame before they will take action. [1] Launching a campaign that will touch prospects only once or twice may do nothing for a brand or product. In fact, it may hurt your cause, because you may attract attention at the get-go but not enough to get prospects to take the next step. Just when a customer is considering your offer, you fade from consciousness, leaving her to question why she even considered you in the first place. It's like ringing a doorbell and running away before the door is answered.

Understanding the level of funding the organization must dedicate to marketing is critical to success. Starting a branding campaign or creating a lead-generation initiative without committing the resources to follow through is not just wasting resources. It's more harmful than helpful.

Additional money for marketing may in fact help reinforce brand, image, demand generation, etc. However, there's also a point at which incremental resources directed toward the same audience are likely to be wasted or even harmful. Most of us don't appreciate being bombarded with incessant messages, even from brands we like. As an example, ongoing exposure to the ubiquitous Geico gecko means most of us know that fifteen minutes will save us 15 percent on our car insurance. Yet I regularly hear people say, "I'm so sick of those commercials. Next time I need car insurance, I'm going anywhere but Geico."

The sad part is they'll likely ask another insurance provider if they can help save 15 percent on car insurance. Geico has drilled the message into our heads (likely cutting margins for all big auto insurers in the process), but alienated many potential customers with nonstop exposure. In fact, Esurance has recently taken its cue from Geico with ads that tout fifteen minutes as too long—they'll save you money in seven and a half minutes.

Marketing resources fall into two buckets: program dollars—spent on everything from advertising to social media to e-mail campaigns—and head count—spent on the people and agencies to manage those campaigns. These two categories are not mutually exclusive, however. Often, the most effective way to allocate resources is to supplement full-time head count with consultants or contractors brought in on a short-term basis to fill a particular need.

Contracting for expertise as needed is particularly effective when dealing with specialized skills or competencies. As a consultant, I'm often brought in to help fill a gap for specific expertise, such as branding and messaging, channel or partner strategy, or market sizing and analysis. The need for this skill at that particular time is usually both important and acute. However, it's unlikely that the organization needs someone with this set of competencies full time once that particular project is complete.

In this situation, using program dollars to "rent" rather than "buy" full-time head count makes the most sense, and it is actually more economical in the long term. Yet I still see organizations with an NIH (not invented here) mentality: "We have great people here—why do we need outside help?" Chances are, even if you have an outstanding team of people, they're limited in what else they can take on. They can't do everything, and they certainly can't do everything really well. Furthermore, great people love working with other great people. Getting a new perspective can be just the catalyst you need to take your team to the next level.

3. People

Speaking of people, how often do we hear that old axiom "People are our greatest asset?" And how often do we wonder just what that means? Marketing involves managing both creativity and specific projects, driving strategy and execution. There is no ideal profile for a marketing employee, any more than there is an ideal marketing campaign for all organizations, or even for any one organization at all times.

Take the time to understand the capabilities and competencies that will be required to successfully deliver the marketing initiatives required for your organization. Then match this list against current employees. There will be gaps, of course. Identify where existing employees will be able to develop and grow to meet future needs, and where additional resources will be required.

Consider the capabilities that are vital to have within the organization, and which less critical ones can be outsourced or satisfied with external resources. What's defined as a critical need will change over time.

When I worked with Cisco Systems several years ago to help define their key marketing competencies, they referred to these capabilities as core and context. *Core* referred to skills that were integral to the organization and needed to be provided by employees. *Context* related to those things that were supplemental and could be provided by other resources.

What's core and what's context changes over time. For example, there was a time when most marketing teams felt Web design was a critical piece of their marketing and it was important to have Web designers and programmers on their internal team. Today, the feeling is that Web *strategy* is what's key, but the Web design and programming can be outsourced.

Kim DeCarlis says she prefers to hire people who have curiosity and mental agility, "because those are the people who will help you get to places you don't even know you need to go yet." Because so many marketing specialties are so new, it's impossible to find someone who has extensive experience in building marketing programs...and with social media, for example. DeCarlis focuses on finding people who have years of experience but are still curious and unafraid to learn about social media or digital marketing.

As part of the team-building process, marketing leaders will likely come across situations where existing employees have neither the inclination nor the ability to develop the skill set needed for success in the new marketing world. This can result in difficult decisions. These folks are often valued employees who are well liked and respected. But keeping them on board in roles that are no longer needed, or where they are unable to provide appropriate value to the organization, does no one any good. Most of the time, these individuals see the writing on the wall, even if they don't want to admit it publicly. You do these employees a disservice by not addressing the situation honestly. Offer choices for training and development, the opportunity to move to another role in the organization, if one exists, or a severance package if possible.

One of the most difficult situations I faced as a people manager involved a situation in which a longtime employee was reorganized into my group. He was well respected and liked, but it was clear he was not pulling his weight. We explored several options, but it became clear that leaving the organization was the best alternative. We found a way for him to do so on his own terms, but in a fairly quick time frame. On his last day, he thanked me for letting him leave with grace and dignity. He had known all along that he wasn't making the grade and he was thrilled to be relieved of a very stressful situation.

As with any successful function, it's important that people managers understand the strengths and competencies of the marketing team. In today's Big Data/Web-responsive world, marketing functions need analytics and analysis as much as creativity, copywriting, and design. Managing the yin and yang of this type of organization takes skill and patience.

As organizations adopt marketing practices that get above the noise, it's important to ensure that team members have appropriate opportunities to take on big challenges and reap the rewards when they succeed. Respect and recognition—both internally and among their peers in the market or industry—are important to marketing contributors, and may be more important to them than any financial incentive you could offer.

It's important to have a common language throughout the organization. In many cases, this will be driven by the culture of the organization. Facebook, for example, talks about hackathons. Commune Hotels talks about transforming the human experience.

It's also important to extend this common language to marketing. I've seen differing definitions for prospects versus suspects versus leads. What's important is that you are consistent within your organization. Everyone, throughout marketing and all the other groups that are impacted by marketing initiatives, should know what you mean by each term.

It's important to understand your core needs and have a plan to cover these in the future. What's changing? How will you meet your objectives? What will you do with valued employees who no longer have the skill set or experience for your future organization? How will you handle these situations?

Coaching Champions

Everyone needs a coach—even Olympic athletes or star performers. A coach builds on strengths—cutting a split second here or there, improving a jump shot. A coach will help negate glaring weaknesses, but no coach worth his salt is going to waste time focusing on the batting skills of an elite pitcher or the punting ability of a star quarterback.

Knowing your weaknesses is important, however, if only so you can avoid putting yourself in a situation where they will expose you and the organization to potential harm. According to talent expert Roberta Matuson, it's important to look at each person as an individual. It makes no sense to take a highly analytical person and try to transform her into a strong communicator. Instead, appreciate the diversity of the team and leverage that. Don't give the person responsible for analytics the task of addressing the senior leadership team and presenting findings—unless she really expresses the desire to move in this direction. And, if that's the case, give the employee a coach so she can learn to communicate with confidence.

Matuson counsels that you don't need a lot of people when you have top talent. Don't take a more junior person when what you really need is someone who has senior experience or outstanding creativity. No, it's not cheap. But it will cost you less in the end to hire stellar, more senior, people. In fact, Matuson says, hire people who are better than you. When your people shine, you shine more brightly.

DeCarlis agrees. "One of the best things you can do is bring together a smart group of people and let them co-create," she says. "One of the things I've learned to do as a leader is say, hey, this is kind of a crazy idea, I haven't thought it much through—let's build on it."

---

4. Technology

Technology has transformed marketing execution dramatically. We have novel and incremental ways to get messages in front of prospective customers. We also have ways to create customized campaigns and individualized responses, to track and analyze customer behavior, and to offer instant delivery and extensive customer response.

After spending more than two decades in Silicon Valley, I feel confident telling you that when it comes to technology, only two things are certain. First, what we have today is far beyond what we had yesterday. Second, what we will have tomorrow will be far beyond what we have today.

The capabilities of products like Salesforce.com, Marketo, or Eloqua can be overwhelming—particularly for organizations that have existing, ongoing ways of managing marketing initiatives. This is like going to an all-you-can-eat buffet with the goal of really eating it all. You're going to make yourself sick. Instead, focus on "eating" one course at a time, digesting that, then adding other functionality later.

How many organizations can afford to stop using their existing systems long enough to start from scratch with new technology? Probably not many. It's like trying to rebuild an airplane while in flight. Yet what happens when today's technology is outdated or superseded in just a short time?

Think of Goldilocks: one bowl of porridge was too hot, the other too cold. One bed was too big, the other too small. Technology investments should be like her ultimate solution—something that fits "just right." There's no simple answer, except to remember that long-term solutions start with short-term first steps. Don't try to swallow the elephant whole. Look at those capabilities that are most critical and find a way to implement them in stages. Be sure to run old and new systems in parallel for a significant period of time, so there's a backup system in case the transition is not as smooth as planned.

One of the most important aspects of managing marketing technology is to have effective decision-making processes in place. Ask your team:

- What are the critical, must-have issues we need to solve?
- Where does it make sense to stick with existing systems, rather than moving to new technology with future growth potential?
- Who will use these systems, and what are their needs and concerns?
- How will we manage the transitions and conversions to maintain business continuity?
- If things go well, what should we be prepared for?
- If things *don't* go as planned, what are the consequences?
- What's our plan B? How about Plan C?

Remember, just because you *can,* doesn't mean you *should.* Be wary of the desire to chase the newest technology, the latest bright, shiny object. Before jumping onto a new platform or implementing a new tool, be sure you understand not just the promised benefits but the costs and risks. What happens if the tool or provider goes away? Not all exciting start-ups survive and become established platforms, despite their efforts to convince you otherwise! What security measures are in place for your data? How easy is it to migrate to another platform or to connect to other tools?

Make sure that your tools and technology are easily available and accessible to your marketing users. It's critical that they're understandable by mere mortals. It shouldn't take an advanced degree to understand how to add or analyze data in a marketing automation system. It should be simple for those who need reports and updates to get to them, and for those who receive the reports to understand what they show.

Most importantly, be sure that you implement tools and technology in service of business goals—not just for technology's sake. Take the time to find the solution that's as close as you can get to "just right."

5. Environment

The last factor is one that many organizations choose not to address in depth, but understanding the long-term market dynamics that impact your environment is critical. On the surface, most organizations at least pay lip service to understanding their market. They can tell you who the key competitors are, how fast the market has grown over the last three to five years, and perhaps even what the barriers to entry are for new entrants.

The problem is that everything we thought we knew about the stability and maturity of markets can very quickly be thrown out the window in today's world. Consider the market for taxi transportation in major cities. For decades, this market has appeared to be both mature and well established. Taxi service is usually highly regulated, with a fixed number of cabs licensed in any given location. The limited number of licenses, or medallions, kept away competition. It also ensured the price for resale of medallions would remain quite high—sometimes into the hundreds of thousands of dollars.

As anyone who ever tried to flag down a cab in Manhattan knows, service was often spotty. It could be extremely difficult to find an available taxi, particularly in areas off the beaten path or at busy times, and certainly in the rain. Cab drivers could be surly and often spoke highly accented or limited English.

This all changed in 2010 when a company called Uber began offering a service that connected passengers with vehicles for hire through a simple-to-use mobile app. The app allowed customers to track the progress of their ride on their smartphones as the vehicle made its way toward them.

Uber has expanded to more than seventy-five cities in the United States and to forty countries. In the process, it has thrown to the wind our assumptions about the nature of the local ground transportation business. In mid-2014, Uber raised $1.2 billion in funding, giving the company an $18.2 billion valuation. Yes, that's *billion.*[2]

Airbnb has similarly disrupted the lodging market by allowing individuals to rent out their homes and apartments. A company called Relay-Rides is doing the same thing to the rental car business. In San Francisco, travelers arriving at SFO airport can use RelayRides to rent the cars of travelers who are leaving town. Not only do renters pay less than they would for standard rental cars, but those providing the vehicles are freed from paying for expensive airport parking.

Each of these examples shows what's possible when a newcomer rethinks assumptions about the market environment. Formerly mature and predictable markets are turned upside-down, upsetting the existing participants and creating new ways for competitors to enter and add value.

Winning at market dynamics involves understanding the key attributes of your current market. It also means you need to be prepared to accept the fact that the current status quo might change. You'll need to focus on when and how rapidly these changes might occur. Ask yourself:

- Is your market closed (with few new entrants) or open?
- It is growing or shrinking?
- Is it young or mature?
- How fast is technology being adopted and deployed?
- How mature and established are the key players?
- How competitive is the landscape?
- Is competition on a local, national, or international level?
- To what degree can you expect change to occur, and how rapidly?

Once you really understand the current state of your environment, try to understand how it is likely to change in the future. This means looking outside the box to see who might be the next Uber or Airbnb in your industry. Can you seize the opportunity to be the disrupter? Will you let someone else do the disruption, but be prepared to jump in and offer effective solutions in the new, changed world? Or will you be left at the curbside, like many traditional taxi services, hotels, and rental car companies?

Change is coming—one way or another. As the old saying goes, which would you rather be when change hits your market, the bug or the windshield?

13

Putting It All Together: A Masterful Performance

We started this book with a discussion of George Gershwin's *Rhapsody in Blue.* Let me leave you with a final thought about music. Musicians are trained as solo performers. We first learn the intricacies of our own musical instrument—whether that be flute or violin, trombone or kettle drum, or, in my case, piano. Then we study the music. We learn the notes of a piece of music, as well as the dynamics of the piece (how loudly or softly the music is played). We discover where the music should get more intense and where it should calm down. We become aware of where there might be strange-sounding notes or accents in unusual places.

My piano teacher, Tom LaRatta, often tells me that sometimes you have to go slow to go fast. "Linda," he'll say, "you've got to get the fundamentals down before you can play a piece at a performance tempo. You just can't rush the basics."

Once musicians have mastered their respective parts, then we can come together to play in an ensemble or orchestra. That's where we rely on the conductor. He's the one responsible for deciding what parts of the music to highlight and what to downplay. He ensures the audience hears the melody sing, that the lines of music flow from one to the next, and that the overall performance is memorable.

A great conductor knows the type of sound he wants to evoke. He's also aware of what the piece can sound like if played badly. It takes a combination of individual dedication and hard work on the part of the musicians, together with the vision and leadership of the conductor, to create beautiful music. Without these elements, the result can be more noise than music.

Mastering the Marketing Performance

Great marketing leaders, like great conductors, know the impact they'd like to create. They're aware of what will happen if their teams don't deliver. They know it's up to them to build a strong set of performers that feel empowered to act appropriately. They know that the result will be dependent not just on the individual skills of team members, but also on how they come together to work as a group. They know it's incumbent upon them as leaders to gain the trust and support of the organization, as well as to provide the leadership and direction that sets the stage for the challenges ahead.

Great marketing leaders know that each campaign or initiative may not be perfect, but the team will review what transpired, note where changes should be made, and recalibrate their efforts for continuous improvement. And they know that if they do fail, they'll fail quickly, get up, then go out and face the audience again the next day.

So, as a marketer, how do you achieve this mastery? By now you know my philosophy. One-off individual marketing tactics and knee-jerk reactions to competitors' moves in the marketplace are not the way to go. That approach may work in the short run, but it doesn't bring you sustainable success.

Instead, you need to understand and internalize the eight timeless truths about marketing. The fundamentals aren't changing. You'll need to start with a strategy. Understand your customer. Know your market. Build good-quality products. Create a strong brand for your organization. Find the best way to communicate your value. Work closely with those selling your product. And deliver, track, and analyze your marketing activities so you can improve as you go.

You'll need to be up to speed on today's new realities. Make sure you are leveraging new ways to deliver products. Collect, analyze, and use data effectively. Target your demand-generation activities to your most profitable prospects. Learn how to work closely with the customers who are driving interactions with your brand. Create content to drive conversations and build community with your key audiences. Develop a strategy to use paid, owned, earned, and shared media effectively.

You'll need to overlay the momentum factors. Ensure that marketing gets its rightful seat at the table within your organization. Build support with key executive teams to be successful. (And if you can't build that support, consider taking your career elsewhere!) Secure the budget and resources you'll need to be successful. Draft the right people for your team, then develop and promote them. Use technology to drive competitive advantage—without letting technology drive you.

Finally, make sure you understand the environment in which you compete. Look for ways you can become a disrupter or leverage the work of other disrupters.

Take the Test

To get started, take the Dynamic Market Leverage Assessment at no charge by going to DynamicMarketLeverage.com. This tool will help you evaluate how your organization is addressing each of the eight Dynamic Market Leverage Factors as well as the five momentum factors. From here, you can determine which areas require more attention or energy. Evaluate what you're doing right and where you need to make adjustments.

Not every organization should weight all eight key factors equally. You'll need to decide where you want to expend additional resources, based on your own situation. But don't default to the way things have always been done before. Look at the programs you're currently implementing. Where are these effective? What should you dial down? What should you dial up? Where can you reallocate resources?

FIGURE 13-1: Marketing Efforts Versus Efficiency

The Dynamic Market Leverage Assessment can help start the conversation within your organization about where marketing is today and where you'd like it to be heading in the future. You may want to review some of the chapters in this book to further this discussion. Use this as a means to engage the leaders within your organization in a dialog about where to focus your energy and resources.

A Journey, Not a Destination

If your marketing today isn't where you want it to be, have faith. You're not alone. In 2013, the Marketing2020 study group surveyed more than ten thousand global marketing executives about a range of marketing-related issues. These included whether an organization was able to leverage customer insight, create strong brand purpose, and develop rich customer experience. The group looked at the responses of high-performing versus low-performing organizations. Among the key findings were that most organizations have not yet been able to pull off *all* the key pieces. In fact, they found only half of the higher-performing organizations excel on some of these objectives.[1]

A Word About Failure

Too many organizations tout creativity and innovation as buzzwords for their culture, but when push comes to shove, they are relentless in punishing failure. Some failure is inevitable. Baseball players are enshrined in the Hall of Fame if they get three hits in every ten at-bats throughout a career. Venture capitalists are ecstatic if one in ten start-ups hits it big. We need to accept that not all initiatives will succeed. Rather than scapegoating those involved with efforts that didn't pan out, we need to learn what worked and what didn't so we can apply that learning to the next project.

As I interviewed executives for this book, a powerful theme emerged: that of failing fast. It's not that organizations *wanted* to fail. But those that are getting above the noise understand that innovation brings with it a chance of failure. So they've created cultures that encourage their teams to try new things. In environments where innovation is rewarded, leaders know that not every innovation will be successful. And that's okay with them. But effective leaders want to figure it out quickly. Fail fast and move on.

That means it's important to start small and pilot innovative campaigns first. Fail fast doesn't mean trip on a worldwide stage with millions of dollars at risk. Start small. Learn from the experience. Then decide what comes next.

There are no scapegoats. If you encourage people to go out on a limb, you can't saw the limb off behind them. It's important to correct missteps, but don't look for someone to hang out to dry as an example. Learnings are shared. Best practices are captured and disseminated. That's true not only when projects work right, but also when things don't go as planned.

Finally, it's important to pick yourself up, reengage, and implement again. Marketing is an ongoing process. Marketing above the noise means taking what you've learned and applying it in a smarter, more impactful way in the future.

A Question of Stewardship

In today's world, do we really still need teams of people devoted to marketing? Should we make marketing everyone's job? Some organizations are already replacing the CMO with another title. Others have the marketing function report to a CCO or other group. Still others are taking away titles in general, because, like David Packard suggests, they don't want to restrict marketing to the marketing department.

IT has gone through a similar situation. Today, nearly everyone in a large corporate enterprise has a smartphone or tablet. In some cases, people have more than one. With the advent of cloud computing, employees all have access to more and more computing power, data, and analysis tools. Yet large organizations still need an IT function, perhaps even more today than they did in the past. That's because someone has to be responsible for IT strategy, as well as for keeping the networks and devices functioning on an ongoing basis—in many cases 24-7.

The twenty-first-century marketing function should work in a similar way. Someone needs to define the core message and create the brand assets, then ensure these are available as needed on a global basis. Someone needs to make sure the marketing campaigns are developed and deployed and available for local customization. Someone needs to make sure the right content is available, when and where it's needed. And someone needs to be accountable for measuring these activities. **Someone needs to steward the marketing function.**

You'll meet people who believe that today's marketing decisions should start and stop with data. The problem is that we can't abdicate decision-making responsibility to the analysts. Their job is to dig deep and uncover the hidden gems in the landscape, not to determine whether this is the right business for the organization. Data leads to information, which leads to insights. But even with great insights, we still need people with the right judgment and business acumen to make decisions. Everyone can do marketing, but if no one owns it, who will shepherd the process?

Now, more than ever, we need marketing stewardship. Just as a good orchestra needs a good conductor, we need strong marketing leaders who understand both the business and the craft of marketing. We need these people to be well integrated into the organization so they can tie marketing to the overall objectives of the business. Only then can we help our organizations find their true voice and be heard above the noise.

As a marketing leader, this is where it's up to you. It's time to take the baton and move forward. Seize the opportunity. Stand in front of the audience and make beautiful music.

It's time to go out and get above the noise.

A Final Note

How Are *You* Marketing Above the Noise?

One of the most enjoyable parts of researching and writing this book was the conversations I had with marketing leaders about how they are helping their organizations market above the noise. The more interviews I did, the more interesting stories I uncovered. And I continue to find more fascinating stories as this book goes to press. You can learn more about the organizations profiled here and find out about others that are marketing above the noise at MarketingAbovetheNoise.com. You'll also find additional content on this topic, including trends that are impacting marketers, case studies, and a list of possible pitfalls that can take unsuspecting marketers off key.

What is your organization doing to market above the noise? I'd love to hear your stories and thoughts: e-mail me at linda@popky.com.

Acknowledgments

This book has been a long time coming. For someone who has been writing her whole life, it was a long journey for me to finally produce this book.

You're reading this today because of the incredible support I've received from family, friends, mentors, colleagues, and clients over the last few years. In spite of being known as the consummate list maker, I fear I will inadvertently leave someone off the acknowledgment list. I apologize in advance. Any omissions by no means lessen all of the valuable contributions I received from each and every person who helped me—whether listed by name here or not.

There are three individuals in particular whose support was critical to the creation of this book.

First is my mentor Alan Weiss, the Million Dollar Consultant, who has always provided great, on-target advice—even when I wasn't necessarily ready to hear it. It was Alan who told me that my first sale needed to be to myself. It was Alan who told me I needed to stop being the best-kept secret in marketing. It was Alan who told me I needed to write a commercially published book and I needed to do it now.

And it was Alan who introduced me to the second man I'd like to thank, my agent, John Willig. John is a warm and supportive man with a great knack for seeing the possibility and potential within a book proposal. He took the time to help a first-time author evolve that proposal to a much stronger and more impactful book. All authors should have such a great agent in their corner.

Third is Mark Levy, who has done an incredible job helping me pull out the key concepts from the book, chapter by chapter, and make them much more accessible and powerful. No one needs a marketing expert more than another marketer, and no one needed the invaluable input and direction that Mark provided more than I. The book you are reading is not the book I started out to write. It's a much better one. And, for that, I am very grateful to Mark.

Special thanks to Erika Heilman, Jill Friedlander, Susan Lauzau, Jill Schoenhaut, and all the terrific staff at Bibliomotion. Working with Bibliomotion has been a real pleasure. You are a great example of how to effectively market above the noise.

To Cindi Baldanzi, Steve Hendricks, Matt Machens, and the whole team at Fineline Graphics and Design, for all your support for both me and my clients over the years, and for creating the impactful charts and graphics you see throughout the book.

Thank you to all of the marketers and executives—some current or former clients, some colleagues, some perhaps future clients—who recommended people for me to interview, took the time to talk to me for this book, or reviewed specific sections: Erna Arneson, Marti Barletta, Robbie Kellman Baxter, Meg Bear, Curtis Bingham, Amy Bohutinsky, Tony Cancelosi, Jim Chow, Todd Croom, Craig Davison, Kim DeCarlis, Steve Doran, Marilee Driscoll, Christine Hansen, Steve Johnson, Hillary Jules, Liz Kelly, Niki Leondakis, Rick Levine, David Martin, Janis Machala, Roberta Matuson, Lisa Earle McLeod, Suzanne Mueller, Tia Newcomer, Ed Poll, Simon Potts, Mike Siegel, Amanda Setili, Steve Smith, Polly van der Linde, Michele Vig, and Norma Watenpaugh.

A solo consultant's life can be lonely, unless you have the pleasure of being part of the incredible Alan Weiss global community. I want to thank all of my friends and colleagues in the world of Million Dollar Consulting—my accountability partners, my 627 compatriots, and others who have been in my corner—including Chad Barr, Andrew Bass, Lisa Bing, Curtis Bingham, Stuart Cross, Constance Dierickx, Scott Edinger, Colleen Francis, Roberta Guise, Seth Kahan, Kathy Kingston, Ann Latham, Simma Lieberman, Jennifer Selby Long, Pat Lynch, Roberta Matuson, Lisa Earle McLeod (who insisted in no uncertain terms that I absolutely needed to engage with Mark Levy!), Amanda Setili, Phil Symchych, Wes Trochlil, Libby Wagner, Scott Wintrip, John Weathington, and Val Wright.

My colleague Robbie Kellman Baxter wrote her book on the membership economy at the same time I was writing this one. Robbie provided valuable insights and has been a great sounding board, as well as a friend. At times it felt like we were book-pregnant together. Perhaps we should get our published books together for a playdate?

To everyone in the wonderful Women in Consulting community, on whom I rely often for insight and answers on all kinds of consulting questions, a big thank you. To Michele Bell, Linda Binns, Karin Ellison, Josue Figueroa, Dan Janal, Ron Lee, Maggie Leslie, Adrian Ott, Denise Peck, Randy Peyser, and Sarah Schacht, for all your support during this process. To Jen Berkeley Jackson, for her assistance with creating the Dynamic Marketing Leverage assessment tool. To Lori Prashker-Thomas, for shooting the best photos of me I've ever had taken in my life—what a gift and a spirit you have! And to Denise Brosseau, Sarah Granger, and all the fantastic women of the Authoress group…my comrades in arms.

Thank you also to my dear friends Linda and Bob Abramovitz, Heidy Braverman and David Skinner, Karen Krupen, and Yonah Levenson, who helped keep me relatively sane during this book writing process. And to my piano teachers, most notably Tom LaRatta and Polly van der Linde, for helping me keep music as such an important part of my life.

To my family…my mother, Janet Popky, who has often asked me what it was I really did for a living. Mom—now there's a book that spells it all out. To my dad, Marty Popky, who was always my number-one fan and booster. I wish you could be here to read this, but your spirit is with me always. And to my mother-in-law, Florence Finer, whose support has been ongoing and unwavering. Thank you.

A special thank you to my sister, Judy Popky, an outstanding digital marketer in her own right, who has provided invaluable input and insights throughout the process, introduced me to people like Michele Vig and Mike Siegel, and read through many versions of this book. She even told me the final draft read better than she expected—which, as anyone who knows my sister will tell you, is high praise. I could not have done this without you.

To my dog, Mocha, who reminded me that nothing related to the book was anywhere near as important as our long walk together each afternoon by the San Francisco Bay.

And, finally, to my daughter, Ilana Finer, who inspires me on a daily basis, and who put up with my preoccupation and frequent absences during the long months while this book came to fruition, asking after each writing session if the book was done yet. Yes, Ilana, now it's done.

Notes

Chapter 1

1. "Rhapsody in Blue," Wikipedia, last modified June 25, 2014, http://en.wikipedia.org/wiki/Rhapsody_in_Blue.
2. Ron Cowen, "George Gershwin He Got Rhythm," *Washington Post* online, November 1998, http://www.washingtonpost.com/wp-srv/national/horizon/nov98/gershwin.htm.
3. "Noise," *Merriam-Webster Dictionary,* http://www.merriam-webster.com/dictionary/noise.

Chapter 2

1. Wagner James Au, "Second Life Turns 10: What It Did Wrong, and Why It May Have Its Own Second Life," *GigaOm,* June 23, 2013, http:/gigaom.com/2013/06/23/second-life-turns-10-what-it-did-wrong-and-why-it-will-have-its-own-second-life/.
2. "Did You Know 2013" (video), Blognology.com, http://www.youtube.com/watch?v=iEz46yhUwuM.
3. Richard Lawler, "Apple iPad Sales Topped 100 Million Two Weeks Ago," Engadget.com, updated October 23, 2012, http//:www.engadget.com/2012/10/23/apple-ipad-sales-100-million/.
4. Sam Costello, "What Are iPad Sales All Time?," About.com, updated June 4, 2014, http://ipod.about/com/od/ipadmodelsandterms/f/ipad-sales-to-date.htm.
5. Soham Chatterjee, "Apple Sells More Than 10 Million New iPhones in First Three Days," Reuters.com, September 22, 2014, http://www.reuters.com/article/2014/09/22/us-apple-iphone-idUSKCN0HH1Q120140922.

6. "Facts About Email," Facts Column, accessed July 7, 2014, http://www.facts column.com/facts-about-email.html.

7. "Twitter Statistics," StatisticBrain, revised July, 1, 2014, http://www.statistic brain.com/twitter-statistics/.

8. Dan Farber, "Google Search Scratches Its Brain 500 Million Times a Day," C/Net, updated May 13, 2013, http://www.cnet.com/news/google-search -scratches-its-brain-500-million-times-a-day/.

9. Om Malik, "Man and His Machines," *Fast Company*, July/August 2014, 36.

10. Laurie Segall, "Digital Music Sales Top Physical Sales," CNN Money, updated January 5, 2012, http://money.cnn.com/2012/01/05/technology/digital_music _sales/.

11. Ben Sisario, "Downloads in Decline As Streamed Music Soars," *New York Times* online, updated July 3, 2014, http://www.newyorktimes.com/2014/07/04/ business/media/sharp-rise-seen-in-music-streaming-as-cd-sales-and downloads-plummet.htm.

12. Jason Abbruzzese, "Internet Ad Spending Beat Broadcast TV for First Time Last Year," Mashable Business, April 10, 2014, http://mashable.com/2014/ 04/10/mobile-surge-internet-beats-tv/.

Chapter 4

1. Mark A. Breyer and Douglas Laney, *The Importance of 'Big Data': A Definition,* Gartner, June 21, 2012.

2. Laura Kolodny, "How Consumers Are Using Big Data," *Wall Street Journal*, Monday, March 24, 2014.

3. "Health Care's Big-Data Boosters," *Fast Company,* June 2014, 103.

4. Rick Levine, Christopher Locke, Doc Searls, and David Weinberger, *The Cluetrain Manifesto: The End of Business As Usual: Tenth Anniversary Edition* (New York: Basic Books, 2009).

5. Mitch Joel, "20 Best Marketing Books of All Time," *Six Pixels of Separation— The Blog,* October 31, 2013, http://www.twistimage.com/blog/archives/ 20-best-marketing-books-of-all-time/?utm_source=feedburner.

6. American Express OPEN Network, https://www.americanexpress.com/us/small -business/openforum/explore/.

7. Laura Ramos, "Most B2B Marketers Struggle to Create Engaging Content," *The Forrester Blog for Marketing Leadership Professionals,* July 16, 2014, http:// blogs.forrester.com/laura_ramos/14-07-16-most_b2b_marketers_struggle _to_create_engaging_content.

8. Ramos, "Most B2B Marketers Struggle."

9. Lee Odden, "Paid, Earned, Owned and Shared Media—What's Your Online Marketing Media Mix?" *TopRank Online Marketing Blog,* accessed July 1, 2014, http://www.toprankblog.com/2011/07/online-marketing-media-mix/.

10. John Lusk, "How to Define and Use Paid, Owned and Earned Media," *Huffington Post,* updated January 21, 2014, http://www.huffingtonpost.com/john-lusk/how-to-define-and-use-pai_b_4634005.html.

11. Odden, "Paid, Earned, Owned and Shared Media."

12. "Nielsen: Earned Advertising Remains Most Credible Among Consumers: Trust in Owned Advertising on the Rise," Nielsen Holdings, September 17, 2013, http://www.nielsen.com/content/corporate/us/en/press-room/2013/nielsen-earned-advertising-remains-most-credible-among-consumer.html.

13. "Nielsen," Nielsen Holdings.

Chapter 5

1. "About Us," ZapposInsights.com, accessed July 3, 2014. http://www.zapposinsights.com/about.

Chapter 6

1. Stuart Elliot, "Tropicana Discovers Some Buyers Are Passionate About Packaging," *New York Times,* updated February 23, 2009, http://www.nytimes.com/2009/02/23/business/media/23adcol.html?pagewanted=all&_r=0.

2. Natalie Zmuda, "Filling in the Gap of a Rebranding Disaster: How Retailer Went from Safe Territory to Danger Zone in Quest for Change," *Advertising Age,* updated October 8, 2010, http://adage.com/article/news/branding-gap-s-logo-change-disaster/146525/.

3. Nat Ives and Rupal Parekh, "Marketers Jump on Super Bowl Blackout with Real-Time Twitter Campaigns: Social-Media Teams at Oreo, Audi, Tide and VW React Swiftly," AdAge.com, February 3, 2013, http://adage.com/article/special-report-super-bowl/marketers-jump-super-bowl-blackout-twitter/239575.

4. David Wallis, "Komen Foundation Struggles to Regain Wide Support," *New York Times,* November 9, 2012, online edition, http://www.nytimes.com/2012/11/09/giving/komen-foundation-works-to-regain-support-after-planned-parenthood-controversy.html?pagewanted=all&_r=0.

5. "Scandal Rocks America's Support for Susan G. Komen for the Cure, According to 23rd Annual Harris Poll EquiTrend Study," Harris Interactive, news release, March 27, 2012.

6. "Komen Foundation Restores Funding for Breast Cancer Screenings at Planned Parenthood Health Centers," Planned Parenthood, updated February 3, 2012, http://www.plannedparenthood.org/about-us/newsroom/komen-foundation -restores-funding-for-breat-cancer-screenings-at-planned-parenthood-health -centers.

7. Jennifer Reingold, "JC Penney: How to Fail in Business While Really, Really Trying," *Fortune*, April 7, 2014, 80–90.

8. Reingold, "JC Penney."

9. Reingold, "JC Penney."

10. Kusum Ailawadi, "The Reason for Ron Johnson's JC Penney Fiasco," *US News and World Report* online, April 12, 2013, http://www.usnews.com/ opinion/blogs/economic-intelligence/2013/04/12/why-jc-penny-failed -under-ron-johnson.

11. Ailawadi, "The Reason for Ron Johnson's JC Penney Fiasco."

12. Kim Bhasin, "This J.C. Penney Worker Was Fired for Telling the Truth About Its 'Fake' Prices," *Huffington Post,* March 19, 2014, http://www.huffington post.com/2014/03/19/jcpenney-prices_n_4986649.html.

13. Bhasin, "This J.C. Penney Worker Was Fired."

14. Stephanie Strom, "CVS Vows to Quit Selling Tobacco Products," *New York Times,* February 4, 2014, http://www.nytimes.com/2014/02/06/business/ cvs-plans-to-end-sales-of-tobacco-products-by-october.html?_r=0.

Chapter 7

1. "About LinkedIn," LinkedIn, http://press.linkedin.com/about, accessed July 5, 2014.

2. "B2B Marketing Budgets to Increase by 6% in 2014," Forrester Research, January 21, 2014, http://www.forrester.com/B2B+Marketing+Budgets+To+Incr ease+By+6+In+2014/-/E-PRE6644.

Chapter 8

1. Daniel Pink, *To Sell Is Human: The Surprising Truth About Moving Others* (New York: Riverhead Books, 2012), 63.

2. Lisa Earle McLeod, *Selling with Noble Purpose: How to Drive Revenue and Do Work That Makes You Proud* (New York: John Wiley, 2013).

3. Aditya Joshi and Eduardo Gimenez, "Decision-Driven Marketing," *Harvard Business Review,* July–August 2014, 65–71.

4. Joshi and Gimenez, "Decision-Driven Marketing."

5. Chris Coppe, "The Three Numbers You Need to Know…" e-mail blast from Marketo, Inc., February 7, 2014.

Chapter 9

1. Jody Sarno, "In the Age of the Customer, Insight Isn't Enough," Forrester Research, June 4, 2014. https://www.forrester.com/In+The+Age+Of+The+ Customer+Insight+Isnt+Enough/fulltext/-/E-RES114843?aid=AST974245# AST974245.

2. Lauren Hepler, "Inside the 49ers' Fan Data Playbook: How Catering to Fans Can Make Teams Money," *Silicon Valley Business Journal*, July 25, 2014, http://www.bizjournals.com/sanjose/print-edition/2014/07/25/49ers-open -fan-data-playbook-seeking-more-loyalty.html?ana=sm_sjo_upc38&b=1406 229725^15051141&page=all.

3. Lisa Arthur, "Five Years from Now, CMOs Will Spend More on IT Than CIOs Do," Forbes.com, February 8, 2012, http://www.forbes.com/sites/lisaarthur/ 2012/02/08/five-years-from-now-cmos-will-spend-more-on-it-than-cios-do/.

4. Sarno, "In the Age of the Customer."

5. Sarno, "In the Age of the Customer."

Chapter 11

1. Art Swift, "Americans Say Social Media Have Little Sway on Purchases," Gallup Economy, June 23, 2014, http://www.gallup.com/poll/171785/americans -say-social-media-little-effect-buying-decisions.aspx.

2. Swift, "Americans Say."

3. Laura Kolodny, "How Consumers Are Using Big Data," *Wall Street Journal*, Monday, March 24, 2014.

4. Kolodny, "How Consumers Are Using Big Data."

5. "Facebook Statistics," StatisticBrain, revised January 1, 2014, http//www .statisticbrain.com/facebook-statistics/.

6. Peter Bale, "Eric Schmidt Shows What Media Companies Can Learn From Google," TheMediaBriefing.com, September 1, 2011, http://www.themedia briefing.com/article/eric-schmidt-shows-what-media-companies-can-learn -from-google

7. The Medium Is the Message," Wikipedia, http://en.wikipedia.org/wiki/The _medium_is_the_message, last modified June 16, 2014.

Chapter 12

1. Laurie Beasley and Tom Judge, *Why It Takes 7 to 13+ Touches to Generate a Qualified B2B Sales Lead Today: A Hands-On Guide,* white paper, Beasley Direct Marketing, 2014.

2. Hannah Kuchler, "Uber Value Hits $18.2bn on Fundraising," *Financial Times,* June 6, 2014, http://www.ft.com/cms/s/0/639364b2-eda1-11e3-8a00 -00144feabdc0.html#axzz36cfnH76.

Chapter 13

1. Marc de Swaan Arons, Frank van den Driest, and Keith Weed, "The Ultimate Marketing Machine," *Harvard Business Review,* July–August 2014, 55–63.

References

Abbruzzese, Jason. "Internet Ad Spending Beat Broadcast TV for First Time Last Year." Mashable Business. April 10, 2014. http://mashable.com/2014/04/10/mobile-surge-internet-beats-tv/.

About.com. "What are iPad Sales All Time?" Updated June 4, 2014. http://ipod.about/com/od/ipadmodelsandterms/f/ipad-sales-to-date.htm.

Ailawadi, Kusum. "The Reason for Ron Johnson's JC Penney Fiasco." *US News and World Report* online, April 12, 2013. http://www.usnews.com/opinion/blogs/economic-intelligence/2013/04/12/why-jc-penny-failed-under-ron-johnson.

American Express OPEN Network. https://www.americanexpress.com/us/small-business/openforum/explore/.

Arons, Marc de Swaan, Frank van den Driest, and Keith Weed. "The Ultimate Marketing Machine." *Harvard Business Review,* July–August 2014.

Arthur, Lisa. "Five Years from Now, CMOs Will Spend More on IT Than CIOs Do." Forbes.com. February 8, 2012. http://www.forbes.com/sites/lisaarthur/2012/02/08/five-years-from-now-cmos-will-spend-more-on-it-than-cios-do/.

Au, Wagner James. "Second Life Turns 10: What It Did Wrong, and Why It May Have Its Own Second Life." GigaOm. June 23, 2013. http:/gigaom.com/2013/06/23/second-life-turns-10-what-it-did-wrong-and-why-it-will-have-its-own-second-life/.

Bale, Peter. "Eric Schmidt Shows What Media Companies Can Learn From Google," TheMediaBriefing.com, September 1, 2011. http://www.themediabriefing.com/article/eric-schmidt-shows-what-media-companies-can-learn-from-google

Beasley Direct Marketing. *Why It Takes 7 to 13+ Touches to Generate a Qualified B2B Sales Lead Today: A Hands-On Guide.* Beasley Direct Marketing, Inc. 2014.

Bhasin, Kim. "This J.C. Penney Worker Was Fired for Telling the Truth About Its 'Fake' Prices." *Huffington Post,* March 19, 2014. http://www.huffingtonpost.com/2014/03/19/jcpenney-prices_n_4986649.html.

Blognology.com. "Did You Know 2013" (video). http://www.youtube.com/watch?v=iEz46yhUwuM.

Breyer, Mark A., and Douglas Laney. *The Importance of 'Big Data': A Definition.* Gartner. June 21, 2012.

Chatterjee, Soham. "Apple sells more than 10 million new iPhones in first 3 days," Reuters.com, September 22, 2014. http://www.reuters.com/article/2014/09/22/us-apple-iphone-idUSKCN0HH1Q120140922

CNN Money. "Digital Music Sales Top Physical Sales." Updated January 5, 2012. http://money.cnn.com/201201/05/technology/digital_music_sales.

Coppe, Chris. "The Three Numbers You Need to Know…" email blast from Marketo, Inc. February 7, 2014. Corcoran, Sean. "Defining Earned, Owned and Paid Media." *Forrester Blogs,* updated December 16, 2009. http://blogs.forrester.com/interactive_marketing/2009/12/defining-earned-owned-and-paid-media.htm.

Cowen, Ron. "George Gershwin: He Got Rhythm." *Washington Post* online, November 1998. http://www.washingtonpost.com/wp-srv/national/horizon/nov98/gershwin.htm.

Sisario, Ben. "Downloads in Decline as Streamed Music Soars," *New York Times* online, updated July 3, 2014. http://www.newyorktimes.com/2014/07/04/business/media/sharp-rise-seen-in-music-streaming-as-cd-sales-and downloads-plummet.html.

Elder, Jeff. "Social Media Fail to Live Up to Early Marketing Hype." *Wall Street Journal,* June 23, 2014.

Elliott, Stuart. "Tropicana Discovers Some Buyers Are Passionate About Packaging." *New York Times,* updated February 23, 2009. http://www.nytimes.com/2009/02/23/business/media/23adcol.html?pagewanted=all&_r=0.

Engadget. "Apple iPad Sales Topped 100 Million Two Weeks Ago." Updated October 23, 2012. http: www.engadget.com/2012/10/23/apple-ipad-sales-100-million/.

Facts Column. "Facts About Email." Accessed July 7, 2014. http:www.factscolumn.com/category/technology.

Farber, Dan. "Google Search Scratches Its Brain 500 Million Times a Day." C/Net. Updated May 13, 2013. http://www.cnet.com/news/google-search-scratches-its-brain-500-million-times-a-day/.

Gallup. "Americans Say Social Media Have Little Sway on Purchases." Gallup Economy. June 23, 2014. http://www.gallup.com/poll/171785/americans-say-social-media-little-effect-buying-decisions.aspx.

Harris Interactive. "Scandal Rocks America's Support for Susan G. Komen for the Cure, According to 23rd Annual Harris Poll EquiTrend Study." March 27, 2012. http://www.harrisinteractive.com/NewsRoom/PressReleases/tabid/446/ctl/ReadCustom%20Default/mid/1506/ArticleId/994/Default.aspx.

Fast Company staff. "Health Care's Big-Data Boosters." *Fast Company,* June 2014.

Hepler, Lauren. "Inside the 49ers' Fan Data Playbook: How Catering to Fans Can Make Teams Money." *Silicon Valley Business Journal*, July 25, 2014. http://www.bizjournals.com/sanjose/print-edition/2014/07/25/49ers-open-fan-data-playbook-seeking-more-loyalty.html?ana=sm_sjo_upc38&b=1406229725^15051141&page=all.

Ives, Nat, and Rupal Parekh. "Marketers Jump on Super Bowl Blackout with Real-Time Twitter Campaigns: Social-Media Teams at Oreo, Audi, Tide and VW React Swiftly." *Advertising Age,* February 3, 2013. http://adage.com/article/special-report-super-bowl/marketers-jump-super-bowl-blackout-twitter/239575.

Joel, Mitch. "20 Best Marketing Books of All Time." *Six Pixels of Separation—The Blog,* October 31, 2013. http://www.twistimage.com/blog/archives/20-best-marketing-books-of-all-time/?utm_source=feedburner.

Joshi, Aditya, and Eduardo Gimenez. "Decision-Driven Marketing." *Harvard Business Review,* July–August 2014, 65–71.

Kolodny, Laura. "How Consumers Are Using Big Data." *Wall Street Journal*, March 24, 2014.

Kuchler, Hannah. "Uber Value Hits $18.2bn on Fundraising." *Financial Times,* June 6, 2014. http://www.ft.com/cms/s/0/639364b2-eda1-11e3-8a00-00144feabdc0.html#axzz36cfnH76.

Levine, Rick, Christopher Locke, Doc Searls, and David Weinberger. *The Cluetrain Manifesto: The End of Business as Usual: Tenth Anniversary Edition.* New York: Basic Books, 2009.

LinkedIn. "About LinkedIn." Accessed July 5, 2014. http://press.linkedin.com/about.

Lusk, John. "How to Define and Use Paid, Owned and Earned Media." *Huffington Post,* updated January 21, 2014. http://www.huffingtonpost.com/john-lusk/how-to-define-and-use-pai_b_4634005.html.

Malik, Om. "Man and His Machine." *Fast Company,* July/August 2014.

McLeod, Lisa Earle. *Selling with Noble Purpose: How to Drive Revenue and Do Work That Makes You Proud.* New York: John Wiley, 2013.

Merriam-Webster Dictionary. "Noise"entry. http://www.merriam-webster.com/dictionary/noise.

Nielsen Holdings. "Nielsen: Earned Advertising Remains Most Credible Among Consumers: Trust in Owned Advertising on the Rise." Nielsen.com. September 17, 2013. http://www.nielsen.com/content/corporate/us/en/press-room/2013/nielsen -earned-advertising-remains-most-credible-among-consumer.html.

Odden, Lee. "Paid, Earned, Owned and Shared Media—What's Your Online Marketing Media Mix?" *TopRank Online Marketing Blog,* accessed July 1, 2014. http://www.toprankblog.com/2011/07/online-marketing-media-mix/.

Ott, Adrian. *The 24 Hour Customer: New Rules for Winning in a Time-Starved Always-Connected Economy.* New York: HarperBusiness, 2010.

Pink, Daniel. *To Sell is Human: The Surprising Truth About Moving Others.* New York: Riverhead Books, 2012.

Planned Parenthood. "Komen Foundation Restores Funding for Breast Cancer Screenings at Planned Parenthood Health Centers." Updated February 3, 2012. http:// www.plannedparenthood.org/about-us/newsroom/komen-foundation-restores -funding-for-breat-cancer-screenings-at-planned-parenthood-health-centers.

Ramos, Laura. "Most B2B Marketers Struggle to Create Engaging Content." *The Forrester Blog for Marketing Leadership Professionals,* July 16, 2014. http:// blogs .forrester.com/laura_ramos/14-07-16-most_b2b_marketers_struggle_to_create _engaging_content.

Reingold, Jennifer. "JC Penney: How to Fail in Business While Really, Really Trying." *Fortune*, April 7, 2014.

Sarno, Jody. "In The Age of the Customer, Insight Isn't Enough." Forrester Research. June 4, 2014. https://www.forrester.com/In+The+Age+Of+The+C ustomer+Insight+Isnt+Enough/fulltext/-/E-RES114843?aid=AST974245# AST974245

StatisticBrain. "Facebook Statistics." Revised Jan 1, 2014. http//www.statistic brain.com/facebook-statistics/.

StatisticBrain. "Twitter Statistics." Revised July, 1, 2014. http//www.statisticbrain .com/twitter-statistics/.

Strom, Stephanie. "CVS Vows to Quit Selling Tobacco Products." *New York Times,* February 4, 2014. http://www.nytimes.com/2014/02/06/business/cvs -plans-to-end-sales-of-tobacco-products-by-october.html?_r=0.

Wallis, David. "Komen Foundation Struggles to Regain Wide Support." *New York Times,* November 9, 2012. http://www.nytimes.com/2012/11/09/giving/ komen-foundation-works-to-regain-support-after-planned-parenthood- controversy.html?pagewanted=all&_r=0 Wikipedia. "Rhapsody in Blue" entry. Last modified June 25, 2014. http://en.wikipedia.org/wiki/Rhapsody_in_Blue.

Wikipedia. "The Medium is the Message" entry. Last modified June 16, 2014. http://en.wikipedia.org/wiki/The_medium_is_the_message.

Zappos Insights. "About Us." Zapposinsights.com. Accessed July 3, 2014. http://www.zapposinsights.com/about.

Zmuda, Natalie. "Filling in the Gap of a Rebranding Disaster: How Retailer Went From Safe Territory to Danger Zone in Quest for Change." *Advertising Age,* updated October 8, 2010. http://adage.com/article/news/branding-gap-s-logo-change-disaster/146525/.

Index

Index

About the Author

Award-winning marketing expert **Linda J. Popky**, founder and president of Leverage2Market Associates, transforms organizations through powerful marketing performance. Her clients range from small businesses and consultants to mid-sized companies and large Fortune 500 enterprises. She lives and works in Silicon Valley, where she's been involved with many of the companies who developed and deployed the technologies that have changed the world over the last twenty-five years, including Sun Microsystems, Cisco Systems, NetApp, PayPal, Plantronics, Autodesk, Applied Materials, and others.

A consultant, speaker, and educator, Linda has been named one of the top women of influence in Silicon Valley and inducted into the Million Dollar Consultant® Hall of Fame. She is the past president of Women in Consulting and was the first marketing expert worldwide certified to offer the Private Roster™ Mentoring Program for consultants and entrepreneurs. Linda has taught marketing at San Francisco State University's College of Extended Learning, University of California Santa Cruz Extension in Silicon Valley, and West Virginia University's Integrated Marketing Communications program.

She holds an MBA and a BS in Communications from Boston University. A classically trained pianist, Linda recently released *Night Songs,* a CD of classical piano music.

For more information, visit www.marketingabovethenoise.com or follow Linda on Twitter @popky.